Joy in His Presence

Christian Reflections on Everyday Life

Lily M. Gyldenvand

AUGSBURG Publishing House • Minneapolis

Contents

About This Book

Our gracious, loving heavenly Father is never far from us—and where he is, there is great joy.

The announcement of Jesus' birth into this world was heralded by God's angels as "good news of great joy." From that moment on whenever people have come to know Jesus and have accepted him as God's only begotten Son, born of a woman, there has been great joy.

After the crucifixion with all its horror and disappointment, the risen Lord Jesus appeared to the disciples in the upper room where they were huddled in fear. There he reassured them that he was indeed the Christ, the living Son of God, whom the Scriptures had foretold would suffer, die, and on the third day rise again. There he charged his gathered friends to be his witnesses. Then he blessed them and left. The sorrowing disciples thought they would never see him again!

On that same day Jesus appeared to two men on the road to the village of Emmaus. As he walked with them, Jesus realized they were sad and disappointed because they had hoped that Jesus was the promised one who would redeem the people from their sins. Now, they thought, this was not possible because Jesus was dead.

Patiently Jesus talked with them, reminding them of the Scripture references to the Messiah. He walked with them as far as Emmaus, where the disciples invited Jesus into their home. At the table Jesus broke bread with them, and they realized that this stranger was Jesus himself.

Jesus lives! He is always with us. He waits to hear from us. God has given us the mystical power of prayer by which we can maintain contact with our living Lord. He is always available to walk with us, to give us inspiration, strength, hope, and love.

The assurance that our living Lord is always available is a source of great joy. When we forget that he is with us, we tend to fall into despair. Our problems seem too great for us to bear. In such times we need the assurance of his promise, "Lo, I am with you always, till the close of the age." Whatever happens— the good things and the bad things—we are assured that God is with us. He knows what we are suffering, and he cares. God can change situations, bring healing, wipe away tears. There is always *joy in his presence!*

This little volume is designed to help you find joy in God's presence in your daily life. The business of our lives sometimes robs us of the blessing of God's presence. Even when we neglect him, God continues to pour his blessings into our lives, to provide for us, to guide us, and to keep us safe. Our heavenly Father waits, eager as any parent, to hear from his beloved children.

It is my prayer that the meditations and prayer suggestions in this book will fill you with joy in God's presence, a joy you will express in your daily tasks.

1

Life Is for Living

In his letter to the Romans, the Apostle Paul urges: "Present your bodies as a living sacrifice, holy and acceptable to God" (12:1). Such a sacrifice seems impossible, yet Paul's letter indicates that it can be done.

To present your body as a living sacrifice is to yield yourself and all that you are to God, to let him guide, direct, and motivate everything you do. It is to allow him gradually to transform you into his likeness. This process is called "sanctification," which means being on the way toward the perfection God intends for all his children. Although we were created in his image, the divine image in us has been marred by sin. God wants to restore us to his likeness, but the devil has other ideas. Unfortunately, our own natural tendency is to rebel against God, to let our own ideas dominate our thinking—and to act accordingly.

Paul warned about this in Romans 6:12-14: "Do not, then, allow sin to establish any power over your mortal bodies in making you give way to your lusts. Nor hand over your organs to be, as it were, weapons of evil for the devil's purposes. But, like men rescued from certain death, put yourselves in God's hands as weapons of good for his own purposes" (Phillips).

This is the struggle of life that we are all engaged in constantly. Fortunately, Christ stands ready to help us. Christ has conquered the devil and sheared him of his power. He can direct us along the paths of righteousness. Jesus can keep us safe within the guidelines that God has set for us.

If we have accepted Jesus as our personal Savior, and if we let him guide and direct our steps, our lives will reflect that allegiance. Day by day we can lean on him, allow him to influence our decisions and direct our actions. Then we can walk in love and thoughtful consideration for one another.

In his letter to the Christian congregation in Philippi, Paul offered some good suggestions for living together as Christians. First, we ought to agree with one another. Then we ought never to do things from selfishness or conceit. If we always put the interests and concerns of others ahead of our own, we will do deeds of love for others as a normal response to the love of God that we have experienced in our own lives. We will not complain as we do our work for God with cheerful diligence, rejoicing in the many privileges which are ours as children of the heavenly Father.

Four times, in the middle of his letter to the Philippians, Paul emphasized the importance of rejoicing—actually demonstrating in spirit, word, and action the deep happiness which is the natural expression of a life that is dedicated to the Lord.

At the same time, the Christian life gives evidence of long suffering, tolerance, patience, endurance, lack of anxiety, and gratitude to God the Father, who supports, sustains, and blesses us on our daily walk through life. It is indeed possible to experience "the peace of God which passes all understanding and can keep our hearts and minds in Christ Jesus," as Paul wrote.

We may not even realize what a difference the peace of God can make in our lives until we experience it. Certainly we know the frustration and the difficulties that plague us when we try to do things without God's guidance and help. But Jesus knows what we need, and he is able to supply all things needful in abundance. When we lean on him in trust, we are freed from anxiety, which can be such a paralyzing and inhibiting emotion. Living in Christ, we can obey his will and live each day in perfect trust that he will direct our steps and guard us along the way.

Does this sound unreal? Perhaps—but give it a try. Christ can give us his peace and confidence as we trust him to work through the difficult situations of life. He will provide our needs, protect us along the way, and keep us hopeful and optimistic—but *only if we let him* and turn our anxieties over to him. He has promised he will keep in perfect peace those who focus their hearts and minds upon him. It's worth the risk!

God will not leave us alone to struggle with our problems. If we ask, God will give us the faith to believe his promises and to depend on his sustaining love and protection. But God never forces himself or his gifts on us. He waits for us to ask, then he gives far more than we expect. "God will supply every need of yours according to his riches in glory in Christ Jesus" (Phil. 4:19). All God expects of us is that we live to the praise of the glory of his beloved Son.

Read Ephesians 4:1-14

Thank God for his provision, care, support, and protection. Commit yourself and your needs to him, confident that he cares and will help you in even the most minute details of daily life. He has promised to "supply every need of yours." Believe that he who promises all this can be trusted. He is faithful.

2

Life Is for Loving

Does it shock you that God can be angry? His anger is aroused when we sin, and he is capable of expressing his anger in strong words of denunciation. In Isaiah 1:10-20 he used an angry tone to express his disgust when he spoke about the emptiness of the people's worship practices.

God said he was tired of the greasy smell of the burned flesh of animals offered in sacrifice while he still did not see any evidence of repentance or any turning away from sins. He was displeased with the empty ceremonies of the people who were trampling through the courts of the temple, expecting to earn the favor of God simply by going through the motions of sacrifice when their hearts were not in it.

"Your new moons and your appointed feasts my soul hates; they have become a burden to me, I am weary of bearing them. When you spread forth your hands, I will hide my eyes from you."

It is shocking to read such harsh words coming from our loving heavenly Father. But there they are in Isaiah 1. God had reached the end of his patience with these people, who were only going through the motions of worship; their sacrifices were hollow becauses they were not sincere. So God lashed out in righteous anger: "What to me is the multitude of your sacrifices? I have had enough of burnt offerings. . . . Bring no more vain offerings. . . . I cannot endure iniquity and solemn assembly . . . even though you make many prayers, I will not listen; your hands are full of blood."

God has no patience with artificiality and hypocrisy. There was no evidence of repentance by these people, no change in behavior, no obvious holiness in their attitudes. They were only going through the motions, and this was abhorrent to God.

Do we not need to admit that sometimes our lives are equally devoid of devotion to God, and full of artificial involvements that God may actually abhor? God looks for genuine devotion in our worship. He expects sincere repentance, amended lives, and caring concern for one another.

Isaiah, the courageous prophet, dared to speak for God when the people had become preoccupied with their material prosperity and were giving only lip service to God. His words make us pause to examine ourselves.

It is not too painful to offer something that we *have*—especially when we have an abundance. It is more difficult to offer *ourselves* for service to the Lord and to his hurting people.

The people in Isaiah's time who received this harsh word from the Lord had been ignoring the deprivation and injustices that their neighbors were experiencing. They were blissfully enjoying their own wealth and possessions, with no awareness of others who were suffering and needy.

Do we see ourselves reflected in this picture? Human nature hasn't changed too much over the years!

"Wash yourselves; make yourselves clean," God said. In other words, take a look at yourselves and see how your actions may have soiled you. First repent—then change your ways. Change your attitudes and your behavior. "Cease to do evil, learn to do good; seek justice, correct oppression; defend the fatherless, plead for the widow" (Isa. 1).

God expects us to become socially conscious—aware of our neighbors and their needs.

To be preoccupied with ritualistic worship to the exclusion of concern for the physical and emotional welfare of others—or, on the other hand, to be humanistically concerned for our neighbor's welfare to the neglect of worship with the communion of saints, is to be eccentric and out of balance.

God expects us to worship him, and he also looks for evidence of our loving concern for one another. Without such evidence of love, our liturgical worship becomes only an empty exercise.

Life is for loving—first God and then all his children.

Read Isaiah 1:10-20 and 11:18-20

Ask your heavenly Father to keep you in his loving care this day, to use you in his kingdom to love others as he has loved you. Ask God to show you opportunities to serve in his Spirit. Demonstrate your love for one another by willing service and by sharing your faith in God.

3

Father, Forgive

In a dramatic scene in the old movie *All Quiet on the Western Front,* a frightened soldier dives into a trench to escape the flying bullets. To his surprise he finds the trench already occupied by one of the enemy.

Both soldiers are momentarily startled. Then, in a somewhat delayed reflex action, each of the men lifts his gun, intending to use the bayonet on the other. But one of the men notices that the other is already wounded and bleeding profusely. He puts down his gun, opens his canteen, and offers the wounded soldier a drink of water. After a grateful swallow, the wounded man smiles his thanks, then he fumbles in his pocket and brings out a photograph of his wife, his children, and his mother so he can take one last look at his loved ones before he dies.

Suddenly something wonderful happens. At first the soldier who had leaped into the trench for his own safety had seen only the uniform of the enemy. But when he sees him as a fellow human being who belongs to a family—a man who is loved by his wife, children and parents—the wounded man is no longer an enemy to be feared and destroyed. He is a brother human being who is in pain.

Many persons with whom we rub elbows in our daily experience grate on our nerves. We frankly do not like some of them. We would prefer having no contact with certain people at all. We don't see them as human personalities with their own circle of family and friends. In our temporary encounters we see such persons only as impediments to our own progress, annoyances to be brushed aside. The mobs of people who jostle us as they pass us on the street do not seem to be human beings like ourselves, with emotions and human concerns. At the moment when they contend with us for the right-of-way, we see them only as the occupiers of space around which we must detour. We don't actively dislike them. We just don't know them. So we ignore them as though they were not even there. Only when they get in our way or impede our progress do we become aware of them, and, in that moment, they become an irritant.

Usually we are able to love people who obviously love us and show it. Of course, it helps if they are nice, gentle, lovable persons. We enjoy the people who are good company, who have good manners, and good moral character. But the mobs who crowd us on the street are only a nuisance.

Christ valued *all* persons. He found ways to affirm and help each person he met. He helped them to become better so they might realize their potential in life.

God planted many of his own qualities in the people he created in his image. He also gave us all the freedom to decide for ourselves what we would be and how we would act. All persons have infinite value because all are beloved children of God. But it isn't always easy to recognize that relationship in many people who cross our paths. God demonstrates his love for every human being when he sent Jesus Christ to be one of us, to be a living, breathing example of what we, too, can be if we let God's love motivate our actions.

We tend to fear one another—especially strangers. But Satan is the instigator of the fear, the animosity, and distrust that alienates us from one another. We forget that since every human being is a member of the family of God, then we are sisters and brothers, related by a common Father. We may not all be what God intends that we should be—but we all have the potential, by the grace of God, to become what he expects of his children.

God does not love us because we are so valuable. We are valuable because God loves us. God loves all persons—the enemy, the ugly, the derelict—because all are his sons and daughters created in his image. Some may be temporarily alienated from the heavenly Father because of sin, but they are all yearned for by God who, like the father of the prodigal son, wants every one to come home to him.

At Calvary Jesus was surrounded by an angry mob who waited to see him die. He looked on them from his agonizing position, suspended between heaven and earth, and he saw them as beloved children of God even though at the moment they were twisted and distorted by hatred. From the cross, Jesus grieved for those angry, alienated children of God, pleading, "Father, forgive them for they know not what they do."

Those ten little words spoken by Jesus while he was enduring the pain and ignominy of the cross, give us the secret to making peace: *forgiveness.*

Read Matthew 10:24-33

Ask your heavenly Father for forgiveness for the sins you recognize in your own life. Confess also the sinful thoughts and attitudes that twist and pervert your thinking. Ask God to help you to be more gracious, considerate, and forgiving of others whose lives touch yours. Thank him for friends, family, and neighbors who have encouraged and supported you with love and friendship. They, too, are the children of God who may need to be reminded that he is also their loving Father.

4

How Long, O Lord?

To be honest, most of us may have to admit that we have mixed emotions about the Last Day and the return of the Lord.

When we think about the "Great Judgment Day," we know that we will be judged, and we are not exactly eager for that experience. Deep down inside we know that our spiritual condition is not good. We know what we have done, what thoughts we have harbored, and how much we have neglected by sheer sloth. We know God is not pleased with us, and we fear that when our account is totaled, we will certainly come out on the short end. We think if we could only have a little more time before Jesus comes in judgment, perhaps we might be able to get our lives in better order. Then we would not fear his coming. We might even welcome him.

But, of course, from our Christian education and participation in worship services, we know that God has arranged for our forgiveness through Christ's sacrifice on our behalf. We know all that—but there is still a tinge of fear which is hard to clear out of our minds.

There are times when the pressures and demands on us become so wearisome that we have a momentary desire for the struggles of life to be over. We feel a deep longing for Jesus to return and to take us out of the pressures with which we live.

So our emotional pendulum swings from eager anticipation for Jesus' coming to a bit of apprehension about how he will receive us. The questions persist: Have we done enough? Is our faith really going to be adequate?

When we become anxious about Jesus' return, we forget the marvelous assurances of Scripture—most significant of all may be this very simple promise, "He who believes and is baptized shall be saved."

We learned that in confirmation instruction. It was often repeated in Sunday school and in sermons. Repeatedly we have been assured that God's grace through Jesus Christ is not dependent on our deserving or earning. It is sheer grace and cannot be otherwise. Yet we still feel some apprehension when we consider the return of Jesus to judge the living and the dead.

We know that we are tarnished by our sinful natures and evil desires; we also know about the "washing of regeneration" which cleanses us through baptism, but we still have a lurking fear that maybe our baptismal cleansing may somehow have lost its power over the years.

Occasionally Christians have cried out in their longing, "How long, O Lord?" As time continues to pass and Jesus has not yet appeared, there has been the temptation to abandon hope, even though when we confess our faith in the words of the Apostles' Creed, we reaffirm our confidence in the promise of Jesus' second coming. We live in a tension between hoping for his return and fearing it.

Fortunately, God does not reckon time as we do. "With the Lord one day is as a thousand years, and a thousand years as one day. The Lord is not slow about his promise as some count slowness, but is forebearing toward you, not wishing that any should perish, but that all should reach repentance" (2 Peter 3:8-9).

It may well be because of God's great love for us that he

wants to give us plenty of time to repent, plenty of time to share the Good News with those who have not heard or heeded his call.

Peter wrote, "The day of the Lord will come like a thief, and then the heavens will pass away with a loud noise, and the elements will be dissolved with fire, and the earth and the works that are upon it will be burned up.

"Since all these things are thus to be dissolved, what sort of persons ought you to be in lives of holiness and godliness, waiting for and hastening the coming day of God, because of which the heavens will be kindled and dissolved, and the elements will melt with fire! But according to his promise we wait for new heavens and a new earth in which righteousness dwells. Therefore, beloved, since you wait for these, be zealous to be found by him without spot or blemish, and at peace . . . beware lest you be carried away with the error of lawless men and lose your own stability. But grow in the grace and knowledge of our Lord and Savior Jesus Christ. To him be the glory both now and to the day of eternity. Amen" (2 Peter 3:10-18).

Read 2 Peter 3 and Psalm 90

Invite the Lord Jesus to be your guest. Pray for grace to be sustained in his mercy and love until the day of his appearing. Mindful of his many promises, trust that his love is great enough to cover us all. Turn your fears and apprehensions about the Last Days over to Jesus. Remember God loves and cares for everyone of us with a great, endless, merciful love. He wants everyone to come to the knowledge of the truth and to be saved. Ask God for the grace to live each day in a manner pleasing to him. Allow him to use you to bring this assurance to others who fear the end of the age and the return of the Lord.

5

God Will Forgive

There are at least four things that hinder us from living victorious courageous lives for Christ. All of them fit within the framework of fear: (1) fear of personal inadequacy, (2) fear of making a decision, (3) fear of the opinion of others, and (4) fear of insecurity.

These are very real threats which may be justifiably feared—but not all fear has real causes. Sometimes fear comes out of the imagination, without any basis in fact and reality. But that does not make it any less threatening. In fact, it may be harder to face up to imaginary fears than if they had a recognizable shape or form. But imaginary or not, fear is always debilitating. It warps reason and distorts thinking. Imagination nourishes fear until it grows sometimes to unmanageable proportions. Fear arouses other unsavory emotions such as suspicion, jealousy, and bitterness. Fear encourages us to do foolish and irrational things. Fear is greedy, too, for it is not satisfied with messing up our emotions; it also takes its toll of our physical bodies, causing weakness in the knees, trembling arms, increased temperature, rapid heartbeat, and uneven respiration.

It has always been difficult to understand how Peter could

deny his Lord after three years of sitting at his feet and learning from him. But in spite of his many protests of love and loyalty, when the pressure was on, Peter resorted to deceit in the awful moment when he denied Jesus, not only once but three times, and reinforced his denial with an oath. Public opinion made him so fearful that he lied.

It had been relatively easy to follow Jesus over the Judean hills, to sit under his teaching, to bask in his benevolent presence. But being identified with him when he was being dragged off by the Roman soldiers was too much for Peter. He feared the consequences for himself if he should be identified with Jesus.

Fear of the opinion of others can easily dissuade us from overt testimony of faith in Jesus Christ, and it can deter us from noble purposes. Fear can detach our minds from our bodies and make us do utterly stupid things. It was the lowest point in Peter's life when he denied that he even knew his Lord.

Fortunately Peter realized the enormity of his sin of denial, so he turned in sorrow to repent, hopeful—but not sure—that Jesus would forgive him. It was not too late. Peter's sorrowful repentance became a turning point in his life. Having experienced a need for forgiveness and having been forgiven by Jesus himself, Peter was better able to share the good news of Jesus and his forgiveness with others in similar need. It became a practical learning experience—horrible and shocking as it was. Peter never forgot the experience.

If you were required to put a price tag on your life, what do you think you are worth? At the moment of his denial, Peter was not worth much to himself, but he was still infinitely precious to the Lord. Scripture says that we were made just a little lower than the angels. Jesus told his listeners that the heavenly Father is so loving and cares so personally for every living thing that he has his eye on every sparrow, caring for, feeding, clothing, and protecting each one. Then Jesus asked, "Are you not of much more value than they?" The old spiritual says, "His eye is on the sparrow, and I know he watches me."

There is a little verse that goes something like this:

"Said the sparrow to the robin, 'I would really like to know why these restless human beings rush around and worry so.'

"Said the robin to the sparrow, 'Do you think that it might be that they have no heavenly Father such as cares for you and me?' "

We are certainly not the victims of chance, tossed into the world to fend for ourselves. We are the recipients of the love of the God who made us, and the concern of his beloved Son Jesus Christ, who cared so much he was willing to die for us.

To believe and accept that tremendous assurance is to trust Jesus for time and all eternity.

Read Romans 5

Thank God that he loves us enough to forgive us when we fail him. Be assured that Jesus intercedes for us when we sin if we come to him in sorrow and repentance, asking to be restored to the Father's household of faith. Three times Peter denied his Lord, yet God forgave him even this enormous sin. Forgiveness turned Peter into a new, better, more dedicated believer in his loving heavenly Father. Pray that God might give you a measure of that kind of love as you live day by day in his fellowship and gracious forgiveness. Ask God to help you witness to his love.

6

It's Great to Serve

"It's one of those days!" the waitress muttered as she handed me a menu. While she cleared the dirty dishes left by previous guests, she continued to complain about having only two hands and "after all, how much can one person do?"

She was so irritable, distraught, and harried that I didn't have the heart to mention that she had dropped a well-buttered knife into my lap. I cautiously put it back on the table, mopped the grease off my skirt with a paper napkin, and tried to brighten her day a little by assuring her that I wasn't in a hurry.

It isn't easy to be a waitress. Nor is it easy, I suppose, to be gracious and pleasant when everything seems to go wrong, when there is too much to do, when impatient customers clamor for attention on all sides, and everyone expects immediate service. I have great sympathy for anyone who earns a living by serving the demanding, and often inconsiderate, public. I wouldn't want her job. In fact, the role of a servant is not one most people seek. Serving seems automatically to put one on a lower level than those being served, and this can be shattering to the self-image.

But, according to Paul, being a servant is the ideal for the Christian person. In Philippians he wrote, "Do nothing from selfishness or conceit, but in humility count others better than yourselves. Let each of you look not only to his own interests, but also to the interests of others" (2:3-4).

Many things, including our natural desire to succeed, keep us from wanting to be in a position where we must serve others. Often we do what we do, not to advance the work we have to do, but to advance ourselves. Sometimes our service is performed for the purely selfish reason that it will give us a foothold one rung higher up the ladder of success—or sometimes just because it will pay better.

Our desire for personal prestige is sometimes an even stronger motivation than our desire for wealth. It means a great deal to us to be admired, respected, and esteemed. We like to be known by name, and we take pride in being sought after for advice. We want others to know how important we are. Thus, many of our good deeds are contaminated by selfish ambition.

While concentrating so hard on advancing ourselves, we are likely to collide with others. When we are bent on excelling, surpassing, conquering, or defeating others, we put ourselves in competition with everyone else. Then other people become enemies whom we must overcome.

Even the disciples were not immune to this temptation. There was keen competition among them. When they argued about who was the greatest, Jesus said, "Whoever would be great among you must be your servant." But what Jesus said seemed to them to be completely upside down. Even after three years of close association with the Master, the disciples still found this strange philosophy difficult to understand.

On the night in which he was betrayed, Jesus demonstrated what it means to be a servant. He took a towel and a basin of water and washed the disciples' feet. This shocked them, of course, but they couldn't miss his point. He said, "I have given you an example, that you also should do as I have done to you . . . a servant is not greater than his master" (John 13:15-16).

It seems paradoxical that immediately after this incident

where Jesus performed a slave's duty and identified serving with true greatness, he said, "Now is the Son of Man glorified and in him God is glorified." His willingness to serve and to give of himself did not stop with a humble attitude or with loving deeds of kindness. It went the whole way to the cross, where he sacrificed life itself for the benefit of others.

There may be a key to Jesus' ability to be so humble in the fact that he never lost sight of *who he was.* He was able to demean himself and become nothing because he knew with certainty that he was the Son of God.

Perhaps what makes it so difficult for us to be humble is that we aren't quite sure who we are. We don't really believe that we are the beloved children of God and coheirs with Christ to all the riches and power of heaven. Thus we become so preoccupied with convincing ourselves of our personal worth and so busy proving it to others that we will not risk losing status by becoming humble enough to serve.

Apparently we have forgotten that the same God who in Isaiah 41 says, "You are my servant, I have chosen you and not cast you off," also says in Isaiah 43, "I have redeemed you. I have called you by name, you are mine . . . you are precious in my eyes, and honored, and I love you."

Whatever we are called to do—whether it be serving tables, wielding authority, teaching, typing, or operating a machine—if we can remember *who we are,* follow the example of Jesus, humble ourselves, and serve wherever there are needs, we will achieve true greatness.

Read Isaiah 45:2-5

Thank God for loving you as his special child. Ask him to teach you how to relate to others of his children whose lives touch yours. Ask him for the grace to be gracious and considerate of one another, for Jesus' sake.

Redeemed? Then Say So!

When we were children, my friends and I would visit all the churches in our little town from time to time—especially if something special were going on there. Being from the "staid and proper" Lutheran church, we were especially intrigued by the little group of people who met in a former grocery store on Main Street. These people were so uninhibited and so joyous! What they lacked in furnishings and liturgical elegance was compensated for by their obvious zeal. In this group there was no embarrassment about interjecting a loud and hearty "Praise the Lord!" or a "Hallelujah!" in the midst of the sermon as they happily affirmed the Good News. (In our church no one *ever* interrupted the preacher!)

In the early ministry of Peter and John the two disciples encountered a lame man begging on the street. To his request for money, Peter replied, "I have no silver or gold, but I give you what I have; in the name of Jesus Christ of Nazareth, walk." The man's response was immediate, enthusiastic, and vocal. "And leaping up, he stood and walked and entered the temple with them, walking and leaping and praising God. And all the people . . . were filled with amazement at what had happened to him" (Acts 3:8-10).

All that commotion outside and inside the temple didn't seem to be too disturbing for anyone. After all, a miracle of healing had taken place, and it was worthy of some excitement and celebration!

Indeed a tremendous thing *had* happened. The man could walk again! Naturally he had to try it out. He had to prove to himself, and demonstrate for his friends, that he had been healed. So he stood, he walked, he leaped. What had happened to him was so wonderful that he had to give expression to his joy. While he pranced around, testing and demonstrating his ability to use his legs again, he joyously thanked and praised God for his miraculous healing.

To observe most of us at worship it would seem that nothing of much significance has ever happened. We sit in glum, silent solemnity, rarely displaying any emotional reaction at all to the declaration of the Good News that our souls have been cleansed and healed, that our sins have been forgiven. But something tremendous certainly has happened to us, too, and it ought to be worthy of some excitement.

Most of us trudge through each day, carrying a load of anxiety about the current problems that confront us and a huge measure of concern for the unknown future. Many of us dutifully assume our responsibilities as citizens and church members, but most of the time we don't give any evidence that we are enjoying it, nor is there any indication that we are happy about the privilege of being blessed with health and strength so that we are able to lead full, active lives.

Even in our worship service, there is more gloomy solemnity than rejoicing over the declaration that God has accepted us—just as we are—on the basis of the merits of our Lord and Savior Jesus Christ. And it is his free gift!

What is wrong with us? Perhaps we have never considered what life without the love of God is like. Paul reminds us that without Jesus we would not only be crippled, we would be dead! "And you he made alive, when you were dead through the trespasses and sins. . . . But God, who is rich in mercy, out of the great love with which he loved us, even when we were dead through our trespasses, made us alive together with Christ . . . and this is not your own doing, it is the gift of God" (Eph. 2:1-8).

Is this not something about which to rejoice? Is this not reason to leap for joy, to shout, and to be glad?

In his last conversation with the disciples Jesus told them that he was going to leave them a wonderful legacy: "Peace I leave with you; my peace I give to you; not as the world gives do I give to you. Let not your hearts be troubled, neither let them be afraid. . . . I have said this to you, that in me you may have peace. In the world you have tribulation; but be of good cheer, I have overcome the world" (John 14:27; 16:33).

What a great and wonderful gift! It ought to inspire deep gratitude and genuine joy in us all.

God's Son has made us free to be all that we can be. He has made full satisfaction for all our sins. It is a good reason to be excited, to be joyous, to be deeply grateful to God, who did not withhold his most precious possession, his only begotten Son Jesus Christ, but offered him to be sacrificed to make full satisfaction for all our sins. "Be of good cheer, I have overcome the world."

Read Ephesians 2

Thank God for the way of salvation that he has arranged through Jesus Christ, our Lord. Considering where we might have been with our natural tendency toward sin, God's plan for our salvation is a fantastic plan which requires of us only the willingness to turn to Jesus and to accept him and his free gift of redemption. Confess how you have failed, and ask for his gracious forgiveness. Accept it with thanks and turn the direction of the rest of your life over to his Holy Spirit.

29

So Little Time

Perhaps nothing makes us so conscious of the shortness of time as the death of a young person. When suddenly a child or a youth dies, invariably someone will say, "Isn't that a shame, he had so little time!"

There must have been those who said this about Lazarus too, for he was a young man in the prime of life when he suddenly became ill and died.

When Jesus first heard about his friend's illness, he didn't seem to be in any great hurry to go to him. It seemed almost as though he wasn't concerned about Lazarus or his sisters because he didn't rush right off to be at their side. He stayed right where he was for two more days. When Jesus was ready to go, he went, but he was too late. Lazarus was already dead and buried.

When he finally came, Martha and Mary greeted Jesus with a complaint about his late arrival. Almost petulantly, each of them said to him, "If you had been here, my brother would not have died." They were irritated with Jesus because he had not accommodated himself to their urgency. In other encounters with Jesus they had observed his unusual power. They were sure that if he had only come in time he might have been able to save the life of their brother. But now it was too late. If only he had moved a little faster!

Jesus' timing again came into question when he asked that the tomb be opened. "By this time," Martha protested, "there will be an odor, for he has been dead four days." What possible good could come of this offensive procedure after all this time? But Jesus remained calm. He knew that time was no obstacle to him either because he is the Lord also of time.

Time is a taskmaster. Sometimes it is a burden. Always it is a limitation. We have to grasp our opportunities when they come to us within the rigid framework of time. We are bound by time —but God is not. That is why it is sometimes so difficult for us to understand God's dealings with us. We judge his ability to act on our behalf by our own limited concept of time and space. But these are human limitations that do not restrict God's actions, for God is the controller of time.

Hence Jesus' delay in coming to Lazarus did not reflect any lack of concern. He didn't need to hurry. His ability to bring Lazarus back to life was not dependent on how long he had been in the grave. Jesus, the Lord of life, is in control of all things— including life, death, and time. Jesus used this experience to teach the disciples—and us, too—to trust him, his power, and his timetable.

There is another reference to time in this incident that seems almost not to belong with the story. The disciples questioned the wisdom of Jesus' going back to Judea where the Jews had tried to stone him. To return and expose himself to his enemies a second time seemed to the disciples a sure way to commit suicide. To the disciples' objections, Jesus gave a curious reply, "Are there not twelve hours in the day?"

Perhaps this comment was intended to imply that Jesus was speaking of the "time of opportunity," the available daytime work period when things should be accomplished. There was

31

something important for him to do in Judea, and nothing, not even fear of attack, must deter him from it.

Jesus' strange answer to the disciples may also be a reminder to us that while we are alive, each of us has a daily allotment of time. No matter what happens each day, whether we do a necessary job, whether we suffer persecution, whether we fritter the day away—those twelve hours will move relentlessly on. Nothing can stop time.

Jesus may also have been telling us that there is no need for frantic haste. In each day there is enough time to do what is required for that day. Time cannot be stretched or extended. There is enough time, but there is not too much. Time ought not to be wasted. It is not prudent to borrow tomorrow's concerns and add them to today's problems. To cram each 24-hour segment of time too full will only diminish our effectiveness and lead to frustration.

It is equally unwise to live in the past and to spend today's time either recounting past accomplishments or regretting lost time. Then we may miss out on today's opportunities and lose the twelve hours that we have at hand.

Maybe one reason we often feel rushed and under pressure is that we have put off unto tomorrow what should have been done today. As we let duties pile up unfinished, they become a nagging burden. We find ourselves at the end of each day a little deeper in debt to time. The result is bound to be a harried sense of too much to do, not enough time, and never being caught up.

There are some things that ought to be left undone so that more important things may be accomplished. It takes wise judgment to evaluate the many demands on our time and to allocate it wisely and realistically. Time is a gift of God for which we are accountable. God has planned all things well, and he doesn't shortchange us on time either. Only our own sloth, procrastination, and anxiety can do that. Every one of us has twelve hours in every day. It is enough, if we use it wisely.

Read John 11

Confess that you have let time become a problem when you have either wasted it or tried to cram it too full. Ask God to help you allocate your available time wisely so that nothing really important is neglected.

9

He Is Faithful Who Promised

We put our faith in many things and many people. We trust many things we do not entirely understand—or even see. We depend on the power of electricity, even though we do not know its source, we don't understand how it comes into our homes, and we are not sure how much power is available.

We trust the power of aerodynamics whenever we fly in a plane, even though we do not understand how the air currents can support a fully loaded plane.

We have tremendous confidence in the power of money to do what we want it to do.

We expect our health, strength, and brains to continue to function for us as needed, and we take these marvelous things for granted, expecting them to continue to serve us without interruption.

We regularly depend on many things which we do not really understand. This is one kind of faith.

When Hebrews 11:1 defines faith, it refers to the faith that we can have in the power of God, "Now faith is the assurance of things hoped for, the conviction of things not seen." Our faith finds courage in those two strong words: *assurance* and *conviction.* Unlike the many mechanical gadgets that make life more convenient, God's gift of spiritual faith is always dependable. It never fails or malfunctions. In his Word God has promised to provide for all our needs and to protect us. The Word assures us, "He is faithful who has promised."

Of course we will experience some temporary reversals, and we may sometimes think God has abandoned us. But often after an illness, accident, or other kind of misfortune, we are able to understand why it happened. We live in a sinful world, and accidents do happen. We may suffer for a time, but God, who cares for us individually, can see us through those times, too, if we let him.

Sometimes we must wait a while before God makes his presence known and his power available. Sometimes he withholds his gifts so that we may exert our own efforts, but he never abandons us. If we are patient and persistent in prayer, he will not disappoint us. His answer and his action may not be exactly what we expected, but he will not leave us helpless.

Faith is believing that God is there, that he cares, that he is able, and that he will arrange circumstances in the best possible way for us. God can see the end from the beginning, and we can't. To have faith in God is to trust his judgment, accept his decisions, and wait for his timing—even when the present seems difficult.

Hebrews 11 speaks of the experiences of some of the saints who were given the grace to endure the suffering of being mocked, scourged, and killed. It is amazing to note that whatever happened to those saints, they held firm to their faith in God, convinced that the spirit of Jesus would be with them and would keep them safe for all eternity.

Our practical, earthbound thinking raises doubts when we are called on to put our complete faith in anyone or anything. Hebrews 11 begins with a simple definition which may help us better understand faith: "Now faith means putting our full confidence in the things we hope for, it means being certain of things we cannot see . . . and it is, after all, only by faith that our minds accept as fact that the whole scheme of time and space was created by God's command—that the world which we can see has come into being through principles which are invisible" (Phillips).

Hebrews also tells us what happened to some of the Old Testament saints: Abraham, Isaac, Moses, and others. Even though they did not see the glorious fulfillment of God's promises during their lifetimes, they were convinced that since God is in control, everything they hoped for would eventually become a reality.

We do not know what God has in mind for us. The saints who have gone before us demonstrated a way of faithful trust and confidence in God that we may follow. The same eternal Father who guided them, still controls even the tiniest of the problem situations which plague us.

Sometimes we are impatient with God's apparent slowness. We forget that time is only a human limitation. God will indeed honor his promises—but in his own time and in his own way. He is faithful who has promised! Our faith will be rewarded.

Read Hebrews 10

Ask God for a faith that will not shrink but will hold firm whatever happens. Ask him for the perfect peace that comes with the assurance that God is in control of all the circumstances of life. Thank God for past blessings which you and your family have enjoyed. Ask grace for this day and for God's continuing influence and power in the days to come.

10

Reinforcement

Do you ever feel an overwhelming sense of being "snowed under" with too many things to do and too little time to do it all? A paralyzing feeling of personal inadequacy may make you wish that you could just walk away from it all. As you dash from one obligation to another, frustration increases and seeds of rebellion take root and begin to grow.

At such times, when we truly don't want to add any more responsibilities to the burden we already have, the only thing we can think of is some way to escape. But there are many responsibilities we cannot ignore. We have commitments to home, family, church, and community. From these there is no escape—even when we feel we have no particular talent for what must be done. Sometimes the only "out" from a too full schedule is to neglect some things or give less of ourselves and our time to each responsibility. But then our effectiveness suffers, and our contribution becomes negligible.

What we may need to do is make a few careful choices and try to eliminate some things. There may be areas where we do not make our best contributions. To say "yes" to every request may mean that we will spread ourselves over too many things, and our contribution, as a result, is not worth very much to any of them. If we cannot give our best to a task, we have not served well, and the results will be disappointing for everyone. This is not good stewardship.

When many demands are put upon us, it is difficult to determine where our unique skills and abilities are needed and where our best contributions can be made. It is frustrating to be involved in a project for which you have no aptitude and can really not be helpful. Most people do their best and are the happiest when they feel that the investment of their time and effort is significant to the accomplishment of the task. Of course, we can all do something, but no one should be expected to do *everything*.

If we honestly are "too busy," as we claim (and there are legitimate reasons for refusing to become involved in too many things), then perhaps our excuses will be accepted. But when the "too busy" excuse becomes routine and used too often as a way out, we may be depriving ourselves of the joy of accomplishment and the satisfaction of seeing worthwhile tasks accomplished.

We can usually find good excuses to accommodate the temptation of sheer laziness. Romans 12:11 warns us not to "allow slackness to spoil our work" but to "keep the fires of the Spirit burning, as we do our work for God" (Phillips).

If we are motivated only by the expectation of receiving praise and approval, the service we render is not in the spirit of Christ. He was never brittle or fragile, as we often are. When the pressures were on him, his resilient strength permitted him to move calmly and strongly. The Apostle Paul suggested that we ought to "be strong—not in ourselves, but in the Lord, in the power of his boundless resources" (Eph. 6:10). He was able to appropriate that strength and was, thus, able to do far more than could have been accomplished otherwise. He wrote in Phil. 4:13, "I can do all things in him who strengthens me" and in Phil.

4:19, "My God will supply every need of yours according to his riches in glory in Christ Jesus."

A sense of personal inadequacy is healthy when it keeps us from depending too much on ourselves, but a sense of personal inadequacy can be paralyzing if it becomes the source of self-pity and an excuse to avoid involvement.

When we appropriate God's help, we can tackle almost any kind of task, knowing that he will give us the needed strength and inspiration and he will bless our efforts.

Read Ephesians 6

Pray for strength for the tasks that lie before you. Thank God for opportunities to serve him, to witness to his love, and to be a neighbor who cares. Thank God for the reassuring strength and witness of his holy Word.

Speak Truth

In his letter to the Ephesians Paul described the way Christians live their new lives. These people, who had grown up in paganism, needed to know that many things from the old life did not fit the Christian way.

What Paul says to them about the ideals for Christian living is still appropriate. So easily we forget our Christian ideals and slip into the immoral ways of living that we see around us. A case in point is how carelessly we sometimes handle the truth. We may not deliberately lie, but sometime we evade truth, twist facts, or conveniently forget things. Paul wrote to the Ephesians, "Therefore, putting away falsehood, let every one speak the truth with his neighbor" (Eph. 4:25).

Today we almost expect truth to be sacrificed if it will interfere with profit or convenience. We tolerate—and have even come to expect—what we call "little white lies," so we make allowances for them. We know, for instance, that many of the exaggerations in advertising are not true, so we mentally discount what we see and hear, aware that the truth has been stretched for the sake of making sales. But truth twisted out of shape is still lying—even in advertising.

As individuals, we have little control over advertising honesty or dishonesty, but we can be aware of it and not be fooled by extravagant claims that may not be true.

In our interpersonal relationships we expect honesty and sincerity. We are accountable to God for our own honesty, yet sometimes we stretch the truth a bit or make extravagant—but untrue—statements. Then we expect that if we jokingly admit that we are only exaggerating, our prevarications will be more acceptable. However, if the statements are untrue, they are as wrong as deliberate lies.

We, who live in New Testament times, are obligated to the same moral standards that were taught, lived, and demonstrated by Jesus Christ. There is no excuse for even the "white lies" which we consider to be only harmless evasions of the truth.

Paul makes it clear in Ephesians 4 that Christians live by Christian standards and principles. Of course, such a way of life may not be spectacular, earthshaking, or enviable. According to Paul, the life that is worthy of our calling as Christians who walk in the footsteps of Jesus, is a life that is characterized by such terms as "lowliness, meekness, patience, forbearing one another in love, eager to maintain the unity of the spirit in the bond of peace." That follows the example of our Lord Jesus Christ. To imitate his personal qualities and live up to "the stature of the fulness of Christ" is the ideal for those who would be Christians.

Paul says that if we would be like Jesus, we should have the same kind of spirit and attitude that he had. At all times, and in all situations, Jesus reflected the righteousness and holiness of God. That should also be the spirit of those who claim Jesus as the Lord of their lives.

But the Christlike way is not always the easy way. It calls for total honesty—an ideal which we know we cannot achieve. Paul was realistic. He knew his own human frailty; he knew that he could not reform himself. It would require the grace of God to do that, so at the end of his letter to the Ephesians he admonishes them to be strong—not in themselves, but in the grace of the Lord and in the power of his boundless resources. He admitted that our fight is not against a physical enemy. It is not even against ourselves. Our battle is against the devil, who is a strong and wily enemy. All by ourselves, we are helpless against his power. But God fights on our side, if we let him.

Martin Luther wrote these words about our battle with the devil:

No strength of ours can match his might!
We would be lost, rejected.
But now a champion comes to fight
Whom God himself elected.
You ask who this may be?
The Lord of Hosts is he!
Christ Jesus, mighty Lord,
God's only Son, adored.
He holds the field victorious
(*LBW* 229)

Falsehood, against which Paul warned so strongly, is not only a matter of telling lies. It is every form of deception—everything that is not right, honest and just. Paul's great concern was for the unity of the Christian church. He knew that nothing divides and separates as quickly and decisively as dishonesty. Paul, who knew the Old Testament well, remembered Zechariah 8:16-17: "Speak the truth to one another, render in your gates judgments that are true and make for peace, do not devise evil in your hearts against one another, and love no false oath, for all these things I hate, says the Lord."

Read Ephesians 4:15-31

Pray that God will forgive your times of dishonesty and deceit— even the "little white lies" you have used to evade responsibility

42

and avoid unpleasant or threatening involvements. Thank God right now for his cleansing forgiveness; then find ways to be his instrument today to bring honesty and right into your circle of contacts.

Believe It or Not

Many things in Scripture cause us to raise our eyebrows in disbelief. Many things seem to defy reason, don't seem to fit in with the laws of nature as we know them, and are not consistent with ordinary human experience.

It is difficult, for instance, to accept even a basic doctrine of the Christian church that God came to us in human form in the person of Jesus Christ. And yet the fact that "the Word became flesh and dwelt among us, full of grace and truth" (John 1:14) may be the most important doctrine of the Christian faith.

"Impossible!" protests one who knows the nature of human flesh, but who may not be as familiar with the power of God.

Faith does not draw its convictions and courage only from that which is obvious, provable, or laboratory-tested. Science has difficulty with the incarnation because science normally affirms as fact only that which can be tested and found to square with the laws governing nature. Science wants to be able to duplicate and to validate its data.

This may be why God chose to circumvent his own natural laws and enter into the stream of humanity in a way that only he could.

We need God's gift of faith (the ability to believe in spite of reason) in order to accept that most amazing, but basic, of all of God's actions in his relationship to us. Only by the grace of God can we believe with assurance that God, who created the world and everything in it, would enter into the stream of humanity as an infant and would grow up to be one of us so that he could completely identify with us. Jesus is that Immanuel —God with us.

God's loving concern for his human family found its major expression in the crown prince, Jesus Christ, who came to be our brother, to live among us, to walk with us, to experience what we experience, and to know what it means to be human.

God, whose power brought all things into existence, offers us smaller units of his power in packages that we can appropriate and use. Faith is such a power—though it is by no means a *small* force!

Faith in God changes life completely. It can transform tragedy into glory. It puts the grace of God at our disposal for each day's struggles. It makes it possible for us to "move mountains" that stand in our way. It can sustain us through difficulties and annoyances that plague us from day to day. It gives us the ability to live more nearly according to God's intentions for us.

We say that "seeing is believing." But faith is the evidence of things *not* seen. We see—or will ever see here on earth—only a small portion of all that God has in store for us. But faith brings reality to our belief—even when we do not see it.

As human personalities, with independent and free wills, we have two alternatives: we can believe it—or not. The choice is ours, but the choice has eternal consequences.

The gospel of Jesus Christ is an amazing revelation of the love of God. What we do about it is up to each one of us, because God has dignified us with the freedom of choice.

"To you, therefore who believe, he is precious, but for those who do not believe, 'The very stone which the builders rejected has become the head of the corner,' and 'a stone that will make men stumble, a rock that will make them fall'; for they stumble because they disobey the word, as they were destined to do. But you are a chosen race, a royal priesthood, a holy nation, God's own people, that you may declare the wonderful deeds of him who called you out of darkness into his marvelous light. Once you were no people but now you are God's people; once you had not received mercy but now you have received mercy" (1 Peter 2:7-10).

God does not force himself upon anyone. He gives us the gift of faith, but the choice remains ours: we can believe it—or not.

Read 1 Peter 2

Pray for enlightenment as you read the Scriptures. Ask God for inspiration and understanding. Thank him for preserving the writings of the saints for our teaching and growth. Thank God for your family, your pastors, teachers, and all others who have helped you sustain your faith through sharing of the Word.

13

What Does the Lord Require?

There is something both relaxing and stimulating about arriving for worship early enough to enjoy the quiet, reverent atmosphere in the church. It is good to devote those moments to calming down from the week's pressures to prepare our hearts, minds, and spirits for the worship experience. The inspiring and soothing music, the light filtering through stained-glass windows, the people quietly and reverently entering the pews to bow their heads for a brief personal prayer—all of these things help to create a mood of expectation and wonder.

Isaiah 6 tells about the experience of Isaiah in the temple. Suddenly he saw the Lord sitting on a throne, high and lifted up. There were angels flying around and they were singing, "Holy, holy, holy is the Lord of hosts; the whole earth is full of his glory" (Isa. 6:3).

What a tremendous moment of worship this must have been for Isaiah! Quite likely it was also a moment of terror, for it certainly was not an ordinary experience.

It may be difficult for us to imagine the scene, although the Scriptures tell us that Isaiah was so moved that he just collapsed in a heap on the floor, crying out, "Woe is me! For I am lost; for I am a man of unclean lips!"

It may be difficult for any of us to imagine ourselves in a similar situation—face to face with Almighty God. If we should be in his physical presence as Isaiah was, we might also find it a terrifying and a deeply moving experience, difficult to describe.

Some services begin with the words, "The Lord is in his holy Temple. Let all the earth keep silence before him." These words express the awe Isaiah felt. He was overwhelmed with the glory and wonder of the revelation of God that was granted to him.

As we read this portion of Isaiah 6, we also note that he was suddenly self-conscious about his unclean lips and he confessed that he lived in the midst of a people of unclean lips. In the presence of the holiness of God, we are all sinful and unclean and in need of his cleansing forgiveness.

Perhaps Isaiah's concern about unclean lips—both his and his neighbor's—came from the fact that what we are, what kind of moral principles we hold, and the standards that are important to us usually become obvious when we open our mouths to speak. What we say is usually a revelation of what is in our hearts and minds.

Jesus spoke strongly about the filth that so often spews out of people's mouths. Jesus' words in Matt. 12:34-37 are harsh. They were directed toward a group of people that Jesus called a "brood of vipers." (What a terrible description!)

"You brood of vipers," Jesus said, "how can you speak good, when you are evil? For out of the abundance of the heart the mouth speaks." Then Jesus said also, "By your words you will be justified, and by your words you will be condemned."

When Isaiah suddenly found himself in the presence of the Holy God, his first concern was that he was unworthy to be there because he knew himself to be a man of unclean lips. How many persons in today's society would be miserably uncomfortable if they realized that they are *always* in the presence of God, who hears their filthy speech?

Apparently many people today do not realize that they sin with their mouths when they take the name of the Lord in vain and rain curses down on one another. There was once a time when only the crudest, roughest persons seasoned their conversation with profanity. But these days profanity colors the conversation of many apparently genteel women who casually and repeatedly take the name of God in vain in their everyday conversation.

There is, indeed, a vast chasm between us ordinary human beings and the God who is our Creator. In his presence we will be acutely aware of our unworthiness, sinfulness, and uncleanness. Yet we don't seem to realize that we are *always* in the presence of the omnipresent Spirit of God. Our everyday speech should be above reproach. Lest we have forgotten, one of the Ten Commandments is devoted to this important subject, "Thou shalt not take the name of the Lord in vain, for the Lord will not hold him guiltless who takes his name in vain."

The psalmist expressed the awe and wonder he felt in the presence of God when he wrote, "O Lord, our Lord, how majestic is thy name in all the earth!" (Psalm 8:1). As he observed the glory and wonder of creation, the psalmist couldn't resist exclaiming, "O God, who is like thee?"

God made us for fellowship with himself, and he made us only a bit lower than the angels. He has crowned us with glory and honor and has given us dominion over all of creation. He has dignified us with certain responsibilities because we are his beloved children. But we tend to forget our royal heritage, and we live like lost and lonely children who are insecure and uncertain about our status.

Our great Creator is not remote and unreachable. He is a loving Father, who provides for us, nurtures us, protects us, and waits patiently for us to respond to his love. He wants us to live our lives to his praise and glory. He expects us to respond to his generosity with thankfulness.

God's deep love for us is expressed many places in his Word.

For example, in Isaiah 43:4 he says, "You are precious in my eyes, and honored, and I love you."

What blessed assurance to know that the great God of the universe is also our heavenly Father who knows and loves each of us personally! Such an expression of love brings forth a wholehearted response of praise, adoration, thanksgiving, and love.

Read Isaiah 6

Thank God for all evidences of his love and care. Return his great love by loving others whose lives touch yours. Assure God of your willingness to do his will as a beloved child, grateful to your heavenly Father for his endless care and continued blessings.

14

A Vicious Circle

Sometimes we despair over our own behavior. We have good intentions and make good resolutions. We decide that we are going to do things differently, but too soon we forget our good intentions and find ourselves back in the same old rut. Having failed in our efforts at self-reformation, we sink into despair and self-loathing. What's the use? We seemed doomed to fail in our self-improvement program.

If there is any comfort, none of us is alone! The struggle with evil impulses and desires is a universal struggle. Even the Apostle Paul had to confess in a despairing tone, "I can will what is right, but I cannot do it. For I do not do the good I want, but the evil I do not want is what I do" (Rom. 7:18-19). Paul was human, too! Even that great man of God had to admit that he had struggles similar to our own.

Paul wrote, "I find it to be a law that when I want to do right, evil lies close at hand. For I delight in the law of God, in my inmost self, but I see in my members another law at war with the law of my mind and making me captive to the law of sin which dwells in my members" (Rom. 7:21-23).

The power of evil is at work within each one of us. It inspires unworthy thoughts. It motivates us to evil actions. It has such a dominating and demonic power that we are really quite helpless to do much about it by ourselves.

When Paul saw sin clearly at work in his own mind and body, recognizing his own helplessness, he cried out, "O wretched man that I am! Who will deliver me from this body of death?" (Rom. 7:24).

God could do that for him—and he did. God can do the same for each one of us—and he will. We can ask him, trust him, and depend that he will keep us safe from the power of the devil.

The evil impulses that spring unbidden into our hearts and minds baffle us. We truly want to do that which is right and good, but somehow it doesn't work out that way. We may make a start in the right direction, but even our best intentions get twisted and distorted in our actions. We find ourselves thinking and doing evil, sinful, selfish things and finding plenty of good excuses to avoid doing the things which we ought to do. And we feel quite helpless to do anything about it.

We may have a real desire to do the right thing but somehow we don't have the ability to follow through on our own good intentions. Pride, selfishness, and laziness work together to destroy our best efforts.

Paul wrote of a force at work within the human personality that twists our best intentions around so that we find ourselves doing what we never really intended to do and making excuses to avoid doing what we ought to do. He calls this condition "being held captive to the law of sin." We are as helpless as though we were behind bars or in chains.

So what hope is there for us? What can we do about a "force" that prevents us from doing the good that we want to do? Why are we so fascinated by wrong and evil things? Are we really helpless victims of our own sinful natures?

Paul's answer is, "Thank God there is a way out through Jesus Christ, our Lord" (Rom. 7:25, Phillips).

If Christ is permitted to live in us, then his power and his righteousness, strength, and vitality are readily available to direct, guide, protect, and sustain us.

But the struggle will continue. We will always be tempted and tested by the devil. He does not give up easily. He is always looking for a weak moment when we will forget that we are children of God. When we confidently—and foolishly—depend on our own judgment, strength, and understanding, we become "sitting ducks," wide open for the devil to take a shot at us.

Thank God there is hope. If we take refuge in Jesus and live by his direction, we have the assurance of freedom in Romans 8:1: "No condemnation now hangs over the head of those who are in Jesus Christ" (Phillips).

Read Psalm 107:1-3

Thank God for his constant reassurance of his love, care, and protection. Ask him this day for continued blessings of health, strength, and provision for your physical and spiritual growth.

15

The Vigilant Father

When God put Adam and Eve into the beautiful, productive garden, he assigned them the task of taking care of it so they would continue to have fruit to eat. But God made one restriction—one simple little prohibition. They had permission to enjoy all the fruits of the garden except one. They were not to eat fruit from the tree of the knowledge of good and evil. If they disobeyed this rule and ate the forbidden fruit, they would surely die, God warned.

God, considerate of the possibility of loneliness, had given Adam a woman called Eve, who would be his wife. They lacked nothing. God was very generous. It should have been an idyllic experience—and it was, until the devil tempted the woman to disobey God's instructions. When she also involved Adam in her sin, they were both guilty of disobedience.

It was the devil's first victory. Sin spoiled the perfection of the beautiful, open relationship that had existed between God and his human family.

Later, God gave to Moses the essence of his law in the form of the Ten Commandments, which were engraved on two tablets of stone. These basic rules were the foundation out of which came a more detailed ethical philosophy and pattern for all human conduct.

Having created us in his own image, God further dignified us with free wills so that we could make our own choices. His Commandments were intended to be guides to provide boundaries for our behavior. They were intended to protect us, guide us, and assure us of the good life—not to punish us or keep us from fulfilling our great potential. Although the Ten Commandments do not give us detailed instructions for every step of the way, they do provide basic principles to guide us in determining for ourselves the best way to live our lives.

In Hebrews 8:10 God says, "I will put my laws into their minds, and write them on their hearts, and I will be their God, and they shall be my people." Thus God implanted a sense of right and wrong in every one of us.

Conscience, like an internal radar system, is intended to keep us on the path of righteousness and to help us avoid the pitfalls of sin.

God knows us, inside and out. We cannot hide from him. He knows what we are doing at all times. "Even before a word is on my tongue, O Lord, thou knowest it altogether" (Ps. 139:4). God knows what we are going to say and what we are planning to do—before a word is spoken or a deed is designed. He understands our motives; he follows behind, and he goes before us. His vigilance is reassuring—yet, at the same time, it makes us apprehensive.

Apparently the psalmist did not have much of which to be ashamed, for he seems to be delighted that God has total knowledge of his plans, intentions, and actions.

There are times, no doubt, when we earnestly hope that God does not know what we are thinking and what evil things we are planning. But we really cannot hide anything from our heavenly Father—nor can we escape from him. Yet there is much comfort in the fact that he knows us, is aware of our needs, and is concerned for our personal welfare. He does not ignore us nor let us drift alone through life's difficulties.

It is wonderful—and a bit frightening—that God knows us so intimately that he knows our every thought, impulse, plan, and action. How great it would be if we could respond to this knowledge with the great thankfulness of David, who wrote, "I praise thee for thou art fearful and wonderful" (Psalm 139:14).

Read Psalm 139

Thank God for his loving, fatherly concern for all our daily experiences—even the temptations and pitfalls of each day. Ask him to keep you from falling and to pick you up when you do.

16

Forget It!

How far can you trust your memory? Is your mind a little like a sieve through which many things simply pass and disappear? Do you have to make notes to remember things and then forget to look at the notes?

It is embarrassing when introducing old friends suddenly to find that you can't remember their names. You have probably groaned at such times, "Now my age is really showing!"

Actually, however, aging is only one of many reasons for a memory lapse. Another valid reason may be that you are busy with so many important matters that less demanding things get crowded out of your thinking. Or you may conveniently forget some unpleasant involvements that you subconsciously want to escape. Whatever the underlying reason, it is easy to forget when we are bombarded with a flood of information.

It is always disconcerting to find that you have forgotten something important, but have you ever thought how awful it would be if you *couldn't* forget some things and if you had to go through life carrying the accumulation of everything that your senses have been exposed to over the years? To coin an axiom, "It is more blessed to *forget* than to *regret*." What a burden it would be for us if we could never forget! Thank God that we can rid our conscious mind of some of the unpleasant things that we have observed or experienced over the years! It would be terrible to have to carry forever the reminder of all of our stupid mistakes and foolish errors. The human memory is an amazingly wonderful blessing, but so is the ability to shuck off the things that ought to be forgotten.

Why do certain bad experiences persistently haunt us and disturb our peace of mind? Why do long past insults and embarrassing moments pop unbidden into our thinking to rankle and upset us long after we cannot do a thing about them?

We ought to make an effort to forget past mistakes that have already been rectified and sins that have been forgiven. When God forgives, he forgets. "As far as the east is from the west, so far does he remove our transgressions from us" (Psalm 103:12). In Hebrews 8:12 God says, "I will be merciful toward their iniquities, and I will remember their sins no more." What a wonderful, reassuring promise! How grateful we should be that God will, indeed, wipe our record clean! He is more ready to forget than we are, sometimes. We find it difficult to drop a resentment, forget a hurt, wipe out a bad experience. But it is unhealthy to harbor past sins and resentments, for they tend to fester and sometimes they pop out as unkind, cutting remarks. It is cleansing and freeing to know that when God has forgiven us, he forgets. With his grace, we can accept his forgiveness and forget it!

The Apostle Paul had an unsavory past. He had been an active persecutor of Christians, involved in some bad situations. When he accepted God's forgiveness, he also accepted the grace of forgetting. "Forgetting what lies behind and straining forward to what lies ahead, I press on toward the goal for the prize of the upward call of God in Christ Jesus" (Phil. 3:13-14). The Bible also urges us to "lay aside every weight and sin which clings too closely, and let us run with perseverance the race that is set before us" (Heb. 12:1). Carrying forward our past

58

sins is an intolerable burden—and we don't need to. God forgives and forgets—and we should do likewise.

Having accepted God's gracious forgiveness for our own sins and having forgiven those who have sinned against us, we should also forgive ourselves—and then forget the whole thing!

Read 2 Corinthians 5

Pray the Lord's Prayer and pause to think carefully what you are asking for yourself. Then ask God's forgiveness for your past thoughtlessness and lack of a forgiving spirit toward others. Ask God to bless your family, friends, and neighbors. Ask him in this moment to forgive any sins you might have committed, either consciously or unconsciously, against that special group of people who surround you.

17

Words and the Word

The beautiful language of the Psalms has been an inspiration to generations. God, in his Word, has not chosen to speak to us only in prosaic, utilitarian words. In the Psalms, especially, he has spoken in words that exalt, delight, and charm the reader.

In the Psalms words are used which paint vivid and lovely pictures of God's creation, his care, and his concern for all his beloved created beings. He seems to know which words will speak to our hearts and souls as well as to our minds, and how they will touch us and invoke a response. God's holy Word communicates the beauty and the charm of God's deep and tender love. His Word speaks to our inmost souls and assures us that he is a God of tender compassionate love for the people he has made.

The words of the Psalms seem to soar to heights of elegance as they portray images of beauty and inspire awe for the Creator of it all. In expansive fatherly love, God has provided luxurious natural surroundings for all his creatures—"even the sparrow finds a home, and the swallow a nest for herself, where she may lay her young" (Psalm 84:3). All of nature has its own ways of saying, "Thank you, God, for this wonderful world!"

From the psalms of David, we can see that he appreciated the beauty that God has made for us to enjoy. His poetry and songs celebrate that glory. Praise of God resounds in David's petitions, which sometimes plead, sometimes praise, sometimes exult in sheer joy. The words of the Psalms reflect a loving and confident relationship between our great God and all of his creatures.

In preparation for his important ministry, Jesus retreated to the wilderness alone without sustenance for his body. It was a time of testing, a time for prayer, a time to dedicate all of his spiritual and physical resources to the task of ministry that he saw before him. It also proved to be a time to confront his arch enemy, the devil.

Fully aware of Jesus' physically weakened body after a time of fasting, and thinking that Jesus was both alone and defenseless, the devil chose that time to attack him. But he was outwitted because the encounter (although it came at a time when Jesus was weak with hunger) only strengthened our Lord's conviction to defy the demonic force.

It was the Word of God that sustained Jesus in his time of testing. "It is written," he said to the devil, "man shall not live by bread alone, but by every word that proceeds from the mouth of God" (Matt. 4:5).

In another encounter on a mountaintop, Jesus spoke to a great crowd of people. There it was his opportunity to provide them with the guiding principles of the Sermon on the Mount, that beautiful collection of Jesus' words that can inspire us in our daily walk (Matt. 5–7).

The Word of God is inspiring and beautiful, but it is also a powerful "sword" that can cut and divide. It is a force so much greater than the power of the devil that it can defeat him completely. One of the early translations of the hymn "A mighty fortress is our God" uses the words, " . . . and were the world with devils filled, all watching to devour us, our souls to fear we need not yield, they cannot overpower us. Their dreaded

61

prince no more can harm us as of yore; his rage we can endure, for lo! his doom is sure, a Word shall overthrow him."

In his earthly ministry, Jesus exemplified his teachings by his life. His words and deeds, recorded in the Scriptures, are a faithful guide and inspiration for all who would follow his example and live trusting, God-pleasing, God-fearing lives.

Jesus, the pure in heart, longsuffering, meek God-man, was a peacemaker who endured persecution without complaint. From his example, we can learn to "turn the other cheek." God can give us the courage to do that—and he can even make it possible for us to return kindness and love for insults and hurts.

Jesus' life, teachings, and example were in perfect accord with the will and the Word of God. His Word gives us a pattern for our behavior and instills in us the courage to follow his leading. Truly, Jesus is "The Word become flesh." As we follow his example of patience and longsuffering, and draw on his strength and guidance through reading his Word, we can learn how to live our lives in patient, loving concern for others.

Read John 1:1-18

Ask God to guard and direct your thoughts as he enlightens your understanding of his Word and his will. Thank him for his reassuring promise that he will go with us through each day's trials, tribulations, temptations, and challenges. Trust him to guide and to lead where you should go.

18

Know Who You Are

There was certainly no "poor me" attitude in the humility of Jesus. He never self-consciously denied his talents, skills, and abilities. He never hesitated to offer suffering people whatever he could to help them. He had complete confidence in the heavenly Father to supply their needs and to help them in their distress, and he was a willing servant to help them through their difficulties and a bold witness to tell them about the heavenly Father who could be their comfort and support.

Jesus knew God's ability to change both situations and people. He saw himself as a channel for the grace and power of God to reach those whose lives he touched. He looked on the needy and suffering people and loved them. He helped them to work out their own problems, and he gave them the courage they needed to do it.

In Phil. 2:5-7, Paul says, "Have this mind among yourselves, which you have in Christ Jesus, who, though he was in the form of God, did not count equality with God a thing to be grasped, but emptied himself, taking the form of a servant."

As Christians we cannot shrug off the difficulties and the problems of others as being none of our business. We are expected by our heavenly Father to show our concern for others in the same way that we are concerned for ourselves. We see others as our brothers and sisters, and we don't want them to suffer unjustly or to be deprived of life's basic necessities.

Jesus had the courage to walk right into the problems of other people. In his attitude there was no evidence of a feeling of inferiority or self-degrading. He did not see himself as worthless. Jesus knew who he was. He knew himself to be the Son of God, heir to the kingdom of heaven. Because he was confident in his own identity, he was able to humble himself and not dissipate energies in protecting his identity and reputation.

Jesus never thought of himself first. He always put the needs of others before his own and reached out to the suffering, deprived, or sorrowful with love. We hesitate to get involved in the problems and difficulties of others because we never know how deeply we will be involved, how long it will continue, or what embarrassment it may cause us. When Jesus saw a need, he easily and quickly moved in to help.

"By this we know love, that he laid down his life for us; and we ought to lay down our lives for the brethren. But if any one has the world's goods and sees his brother in need, yet closes his heart against him, how does God's love abide in him? Little children, let us not love in word or speech but in deed and truth" (1 John 3:16-18).

Jesus didn't need to prove who he was. Knowing who he was, he could use his energies for others. Perhaps the essence of real humility is to know who we are, to believe and accept our identity as the beloved children of God. Knowing this, we need never fear we will lose status by being the servant of others.

Knowing *who* we are—and perhaps more importantly—*whose* we are, we can be free to do the will of God in full confidence that he will provide the wisdom and the skills we need.

Read Philippians 2

Thank God that he has made each of us in his image and has provided us with many skills and abilities, many of which we may not yet have discovered. Ask him for the courage to reach out to others with compassion and loving deeds so that all of God's children may enjoy the good life. Trust God to keep you this day and to open opportunities for you to help others. Claim his promises of provision for all your needs. He will not fail us.

19

Be Ready!

Having been present during the horrible events of the cruci-fixion, and having seen Jesus buried in a borrowed tomb, Mary certainly didn't expect to see him again and talk with him on that Sunday morning when she came back to the tomb. But there he was—alive—and when he spoke to her, he gave her a task to do for him: "Go and tell Peter and the others." He didn't need to spell out the rest of the message. She could see for her-self; Jesus, whom she had seen in agony dying on the horrible cross, was standing before her alive. Now he was asking her to share that good news with her friends. In that moment Mary was "ordained" to ministry, called to be a missionary, expected to be a witness. The message she had for her friends was so tremendous that she couldn't wait to get there. She ran quickly to the upper room where the disciples were hiding in fear for their lives.

The words of the "Great Commission" (Matt. 28:18-20) were spoken later by Jesus to the eleven disciples, just before he ascended to heaven. These words are an amplification of the simple directive given to Mary. To the eleven disciples Jesus clearly defined their responsibility to witness. He said, "All

authority in heaven and earth has been given to me. Go therefore and make disciples of all nations, baptizing them in the
name of the Father and of the Son and of the Holy Spirit, teaching them to observe all that I have commanded you; and lo, I
am with you always, to the close of the age."

With these instructions the disciples were ordained to be min-
isters of the gospel of Jesus Christ. But no less important was
the simple instruction to Mary, a lay woman, who knew and
loved Jesus Christ and was convinced of his divinity by the evidence of his resurrection. The message was the same: Jesus is
risen! The fact is the essence of our faith. Jesus was no mere
man. He is the Son of God, with power and authority over life
and death. He is to be worshiped because he is God incarnate,
the Almighty, the everlasting Savior.

When the reality and meaning of Jesus' resurrection from the
dead dawned on Mary, she certainly didn't dilly-dally. She didn't
wonder whether or not she would be able to tell the good news
in fluent words. She didn't question her authority. She didn't
wonder whether or not she was well enough educated for ministry. She didn't have on the tip of her tongue a number of excuses and reasons why she should not be the one to go and tell
the others what she had just seen. Jesus was alive! That was the
good news she had, so she ran quickly to share it.

There have been some reluctant servants whom God had to
convince before they would do what he wanted them to do.
Moses is a good example. He had a number of excuses for not
wanting to go back to Egypt to confront Pharaoh with God's
order that he should release the Israelite hostages. First, he protested, he was not eloquent enough; he wouldn't know what to
say. Does that sound familiar? It is the same answer many of us
give to avoid being a witness to our faith. "I wouldn't know
what to say!" we protest. Then to make that excuse sound more
believable, we add, "I don't know the Scriptures well enough,
and I don't have time, and I get so embarrassed when I have to
speak in public."

67

Why should we be embarrassed to tell someone about the most important event of all history?

God assured Moses that he would be with him on his difficult assignment in Egypt. He said that he would put words in his mouth, and Moses was authorized to preface whatever he said with the words, "Thus says the Lord." This would indicate that he was speaking by the authority and power of God.

It is unlikely that any of us will be called on to witness in a situation like Moses' in Egypt, although many Christians have gone to equally distant and difficult places. But every Christian, wherever he or she is placed, has the responsibility, as Peter wrote, to "be ready at any time to give a quiet and reverent answer to any man who wants a reason for the hope that you have within you" (1 Peter 3:15, Phillips).

Of course, we are not all eloquent. Although we may have great faith, we may not feel we are fluent or have the skill to explain what our faith means to us. Some of us are embarrassed to talk about our deepest feelings. But very naturally, in ordinary conversation with friends, any of us should be able to tell informally what God has done for us, how he has strengthened us and helped us through difficult times, how he has supplied our needs, how he has sustained and blessed us from day to day. Witnessing about our faith in Christ can be as natural as sharing good news about a bargain in a grocery store or telling a friend about an exciting family event.

"We ought to make a sane estimate of our capabilities"—neither exaggerating nor minimizing what we can do. "Through the grace of God we have different gifts. If our gift is preaching, let us preach to the limit of our vision. If it is serving others, let us concentrate on our service; if it is teaching, let us give all we have to our teaching; and if our gift be the stimulating of the faith of others, let us set ourselves to it. Let the one who is called to give, give freely; let the one who wields authority, think of his responsibility; and let the one who feels sympathy for others, act cheerfully" (Rom. 12:6-8, Phillips).

68

Did you notice the variety of gifts mentioned? Paul writes of preaching, serving others, teaching, stimulating the faith of others, giving, using authority, being sympathetic. There is something in that list that every one of us can do, and do well.

Obviously none of us has all the gifts Paul listed in Romans 12. But certainly we all have some gifts by which we can share with others the essence of our personal faith in the goodness of God.

If we care for one another as family or friends, we want the best for each other. If Christ has become the guiding power in your life, you will naturally want to share that source of strength with others who are struggling with the difficulties of life, as you have at times.

Paul reminds us that "Whatever you do, in word or deed, do everything in the name of the Lord Jesus, giving thanks to God the Father through him" (Col. 3:17).

Our influence and how we relate to people around us can be a witness to what we believe about Jesus Christ and how we are living our lives for him. We ought to be ready at all times to give an answer to anyone who asks the reason for the hope that we have. "Your conduct among the surrounding peoples should always be good and right, so that . . . they may glorify God when they see how well you conduct yourself (2 Peter 2:12, Phillips).

Whatever we say or do is some kind of witness. We hope our lives and our conversation will give others a clear understanding that we belong to God by virtue of the grace of our heavenly Father, who has reached out to us in Jesus Christ.

Read Mark 16

Pray for the grace and courage to share, simply and sincerely, what knowing Jesus Christ and his love and forgiveness has meant to you. Thank God every day for his care and concern. Be alert to his gracious gifts and protection and tell others how good he has been.

69

20

To Know Him Is to Love Him

All through the ages people have sought to know God. He has revealed himself in many different ways. Sometimes his actions have caused a response of fear. Sometimes they have aroused a response of love and a desire to serve him.

People have tried to atone for their sins by bringing sacrifices. Led by their priests, they have made a public event of their offerings and there were different kinds of offerings made. Animals were sacrificed on behalf of the entire community. There were peace offerings to assure continued good relations with God, and there were sin offerings to atone for the wrongs of the people. In order to worship properly, there were a great many rules to observe, and it was a heavy burden for the people, because every phase of the observance had to be done strictly in accordance with the laws. There seemed to be much fear and worry about whether or not their sacrifices were pleasing to God and whether the people had done enough.

When the practices in the temple became so bad that the money changers were simply taking over, robbing the people and turning the holy place into shambles, Jesus drove them from the temple with a whip.

In his ministry Jesus tried to help people understand what God really expects from us in response to his love. It is not blood and smoke and burning flesh of animals that God expects. What he really looks for is obedience to his laws, love for one another, evidence of concern and service and sharing.

Jesus said, "If you are offering your gift at the altar, and there remember that your brother has something against you, leave your gift before the altar and go; first be reconciled to your brother, and then come and offer your gift" (Matt. 5:23-24).

Jesus brought this dimension of caring for fairness and justice in human relationships into the lives of worshipers. He wasn't inventing something new. What he was doing was reminding the people of something that had somehow become lost in history. Way back in Isaiah's time God had revealed what he really expected in the way of worship: "Is not this the fast that I choose: to loose the bonds of wickedness, to undo the thongs of the yoke, to let the oppressed go free, and to break every yoke? Is it not to share your bread with the hungry, and bring the homeless poor into your house; when you see the naked, to cover him, and not to hide yourself from your own flesh?" (Isaiah 58:6-7).

It is this everyday kind of relationship with one another in a spirit of caring that is pleasing to God.

Jesus tried to help the people understand that sacrifice and offerings don't mean a thing unless they are accompanied with deeds of love and evidence of concern for the welfare of another.

In Matthew 25 Jesus told the people that on judgment day God will separate people as a shepherd separates the sheep from the goats. The basis for judgment and separation will be whether or not the hungry have been fed and the naked clothed and the imprisoned have been visited. Jesus summed it up by saying, "As you did it to one of the least of these my brethren, you did it to me."

From this it ought to be clear that worship of God has to include concern for the welfare of his children. God depends on us to be his agents of reconciliation and his loving sons and daughters, who will see to it that all the others of his children are able to enjoy the blessings of life too. This means constant alertness to the social situation around us so that none of the children of God suffers from want while others accumulate and hoard the necessities of life.

The worship of God must permeate the total awareness of every person in all human contacts, too. We are "agents of reconciliation," and that means that we also be "agents of distribution" so that God's gifts are shared by all his children.

Read Isaiah 58:6-12

Pray for the grace to share your blessings and goods with others of God's children who suffer from deprivation. Ask him to make you aware of his people who are in need and to give you the grace to be his messenger with both his gracious word of forgiveness and grace and the word of encouragement and material help.

21

Chaos or Control

On a flight into New York the jet liner on which I was a passenger had to go into a "holding pattern." This was not unusual, since traffic both in and out of New York is so heavy that many times incoming planes are "stacked up" for almost an hour waiting their turn to land.

As we made several wide sweeping circles out over the Atlantic Ocean, back over New Jersey, over Manhattan, and out over the ocean again, I could see several other planes making a similar circuit. The delay in landing was annoying, but there was much comfort in the thought that each pilot was meticulously observing instructions to maintain his assigned altitude and was circling his plane within a prescribed arc. I had confidence that none of the pilots would attempt to land until he had proper clearance from the control tower.

I tried not to think about what would happen if any of the pilots should resent being told what to do. I didn't want to contemplate the chaos that would result if one of them should assert his independence and choose to ignore the restrictions placed on him by the people in the control tower. Mature, well-trained pilots know that they can't see the whole situation. They welcome the advice and the guidance of the people in the tower. They know where each plane is, and they are able to direct traffic for the safety of everyone in the area. If there is any place where absolute obedience to orders is important, it certainly is in controlling the traffic of a busy air terminal.

There was minor chaos on the street corner one afternoon when the traffic light blacked out for an hour. The cars and trucks that normally take their turns flowing rapidly through the intersection moved uncertainly in both directions in disorder. No one knew when it was his turn, so there was much screeching of brakes and honking of horns. Pedestrians were equally confused as they watched for a chance to dodge safely through the confusion.

If each of us lived in isolation, we could move freely in whatever direction we would choose. We could make our own rules, or do without them, if we wished. But we are surrounded by people. Wherever there are many people coming and going, there must be controls, and someone has to be responsible for setting limits, for determining precedence, for establishing guidelines to avoid chaos.

Within the family, those best qualified to do this are those who by reason of their maturity and experience see more of the picture. Normally this is the parents.

As the pilot of the plane needs to look to the tower for his directions, so children need to look to their parents for their "flight" plans. If the men in the control tower fail to do their job, the resulting confusion will be terrifying to contemplate. If parents abdicate their responsibility to provide leadership and establish boundaries, there will be chaos, confusion, and maybe even disaster in the family.

Each person is a free agent with innumerable free choices he must make all the time. Our individual freedom is best exercised when it is under some kind of control.

Pilots are carefully trained to function with good judgment in emergencies. Youth, too, must be trained to function responsibly without parental direction and supervision. The freedom that youth is so eager to have will come when they are mature enough to recognize when they may take independent action and when they should seek advice. Like a good pilot they should know the rules and adhere strictly to them. When they mature a little, they will welcome the advice, and even the orders, of those who can see more of the situation.

All of us live within the framework of the larger "family of God." We are all subject to certain disciplines, some of them self-imposed. When Jesus said, "Love one another as I have loved you," he gave us a handy, condensed, pocket rule by which to direct our actions and to evaluate our relationships. The Bible, of course, amplifies and interprets that principle, defining in much finer detail how we ought to live and move. None of us can see the entire picture, but God does. He knows the ultimate results of all of our choices. We are dependent on him to help us determine our "flight pattern." If we are wise enough to recognize our own limitations, we will acknowledge there is always the possibility of a collision with others in our orbit. For our own safety, and that of others, we ought to welcome some guidance.

Controls, rules, discipline and guidance are not the enemies of freedom. They facilitate it. Without control there is chaos, in chaos there is confusion, and that never serves the purposes of individual freedom.

Read Psalm 3:1-11

Thank God that every person whom he has made in his image has also been given a mind and a free will so that each can make choices. Thank God for these gifts of personality. Thank him, too, that when we feel uncertain and insecure about the judgments we need to make, he is there, ready, willing, and eager to give us counsel and advice. Then we can direct our energies into

75

worthy channels. Confess that, as human beings with independent wills, we sometimes tend to try to "do it ourselves," but when we do sometimes we end up in trouble. Thank God for his love and his wisdom. Ask your heavenly Father to guide you safely through the day.

22

Things Not Seen

A statement in Hebrews 11 tells us that faith does not always obtain the things hoped for, nor does it always live long enough to see the things dreamed about accomplished. After mentioning a number of persons who lived their lives "by faith," Hebrews 11:13 says, "these all died in faith, not having received what was promised."

Abraham, for instance, lived his life in expectation of the Promised Land and the Holy City, but he was never permitted to reach those places.

Sarah saw Isaac, the child of her dreams, born into the world in spite of natural limitations, but she was never permitted to see the fulfillment of God's purposes for her miracle child.

Moses struggled and suffered and sacrificed hoping to reach the Promised Land, but he saw it only from a distance, and he never set foot on it.

Joshua never saw the results of his struggle and the birth of the nation, which had been his consuming desire.

David didn't live to see the temple in all its glory.

These persons all "died in faith, not having seen or having received the reality of the promises." That phrase is repeated several times in the Scriptures. One wonders why God took these people home to himself before they were permitted to see that which they had dreamed about and worked for become a reality. Perhaps their faith was so great and so vivid that it seemed to give substance to the things they had hoped for. Their dreams, goals, and ambitions were almost like reality because they had believed so firmly that God would bring them to completion in his own good time. Perhaps this is the real meaning of faith: to be so confident in God's bountifulness that we don't actually need to see the promises fulfilled. He who promised is faithful; he will not fail.

Sometimes we say, "Faith is the victory!" We know that many things happen as a result of faith in God's ability to provide for our needs and to change situations. All of us have experienced some amazing answers to prayers. We know many things that have come to pass because we believed. God does indeed honor his promises—in his own way and in his own time. Many times we have seen what might be called "amazing coincidences, unexpected experiences, special evidences of God's care and concern," but they are really "answers to prayer." Many times we recognize God's action in circumstances that have been almost miraculously rearranged, or when we know we have been kept safe from some threatening danger.

If we do not avail ourselves of God's protective power, we may suffer undue hardships and be poorer in many ways. We are often perplexed, timid, and frustrated because we have failed to ask God for his presence and power in our circumstances. Sometimes God does not seem to respond to our demands or meet our schedule. Later, however, we are able to see that his judgment was far better than ours. When impatiently expecting immediate action, we may not have realized that his power was already at work. When all goes well, we often take the credit for the way things work out for us. Sometimes we even give the credit for good results to fate or good luck— forgetting that God had been directing things all along the way.

Jesus said "Oh, you of little faith!" He was right, of course. We are often more ready to trust what we can see of goodness in other people than to put our confidence in the promises of God. God may already be moving through the problem on our behalf. Sometimes we think the obstacles that loom before us are impossible barricades, so we give up in despair rather than ask God for help. We forget that God can see beyond the obstacles. He can smooth the way for us. His promises are dependable—and they are timeless. He has promised, "All things are possible to him who believes" (Matt. 9:23). But, of course, not all things are good and right, so sometimes God will frustrate our wrong impulses in order to protect us. God's timing is not the same as ours. He sees the end from the beginning. He knows the hazards along the way. We can trust him to lead us—if we will only let him.

We are naturally materialistic. We tend to trust what we can touch, feel, see, and hear. We want to deal with solid, proven facts. We want concrete evidence before we will be convinced. This makes it difficult for us to put our trust in God. We want to see or feel his power working for us. We want to acquire the things we desire; we want to see a situation changed. But we don't always recognize that God actually has done what we wanted—but in his way. Many times, in answer to our prayers, God changes the situation so the threat, the problem, and the hazards are removed. Faith encourages us to go forward in confidence that God, who cares about us, can see beyond the immediate situation to the ultimate result. When he detains us, it is to keep us from stumbling.

Faith that expects our desires to be fulfilled like an order at the shopping center is not faith at its deepest level. The greatest faith is the simple confidence that God cares and will provide what is best for us, in his own good time, and in his own way.

Hebrews 11, after many examples of the fruits of faith, says that some did not receive what was promised because "God had foreseen something better."

Sometimes our prayer requests may be too skimpy. God may not give us what we ask because it is not enough. He is a generous, caring father. He will give us the best, and it will be as much as we can handle.

Read Hebrews 11

Admit that you don't know what is good for you and what may be harmful. Claim God's promise that he will give you what is best. Thank him for his loving care and ask him for patience to wait for his timing. Acknowledge how much you need his care and protection. Speak to God honestly and naturally, as you would speak to your earthly father, asking him to provide for you. Thank God for his goodness; tell him what he means to you and how much you need his continuing love.

23

We Are Loved

It is a good thing that God does not abandon us to our own foolishness, or we would be in deep trouble!

Like headstrong children the people of Israel tried the patience of God over and over again. They deliberately rebelled against the gentle restrictions he put upon them. But even so, God did not give up on them. They were very special to him. Over and over again, God stretched out his hand in loving reassurance that they were a special people, selected for a special purpose in his cosmic plan.

As we read portions of the Old Testament, we can identify with the people's rebellion; they ignored God's laws and found themselves in deep trouble. We do it all the time! Human nature hasn't changed that much.

But God still loves us. In Isaiah 43 God refers to himself as "your Redeemer, the Holy One of Israel, your Savior." "Because," he says, "you are precious in my eyes, and honored and I love you, I give men in return for you, peoples in exchange for your life. Fear not, for I am with you."

What a glorious expression of love! God knows each one of us individually. We know that we are not always very lovable, but the grace of God does not depend on our deserving. The grace of God rises above all evidences to the contrary. Why? Because God is love and he cannot deny his own nature.

God, the loving Father, will never forsake the work of his hands. The psalmist knew that as he wrote, "The Lord will fulfill his purpose for me; thy steadfast love, O Lord, endures forever" (Psalm 138:8).

Scripture is full of assurances that God won't give up on us because we are his own. The Apostle Paul knew this from his own experiences, and he affirmed the fact when he wrote, "I am sure that he who began a good work in you will bring it to completion" (Phil. 1:6).

How can we respond adequately to our loving Lord when we realize that each one of us is the object of the specific love of the great God who made every one and every thing in the vast universe? To contemplate the magnitude of God's love is overwhelming.

God has expressed his love for each of us individually. He calls us to community, to be his church. He asks us to bring together all nations and all people, including the handicapped, so we may let all the world know that we have discovered the glorious truth that we who were created by the Eternal Father are "precious, honored and loved" by that great God.

"You are my witnesses," says the Lord, "and my servant whom I have chosen, that you may know and believe and understand that I am He. Before me no god was formed nor shall there be any after me. I, I am the Lord and besides me there is no other . . . and you are my witnesses" (Isa. 43:10-12).

Our God is a great God, the eternal One, the Creator of all things—but he is also our father who loves us individually as his precious children. He chose to assume human flesh in the person of Jesus Christ so we could know him more personally and be able to appropriate his power to do his will. His Son Jesus Christ walked among us as a brother to help us learn to know our Father God.

There is great comfort in believing that God understands our human condition, that he cares about us very deeply, that he forgives our foolishness—and even our deliberately wicked disobedience, that he will restore to us his good grace, if we repent.

We are his witnesses to tell others what we have learned about him from his loving relationship with us.

Read Isaiah 43:1-10

Thank God for evidences of his love and provision. Take seriously his call to share with others his loving care. Commend yourself and your family to his continuing guidance, protection, and love.

24

What's in a Name?

We have social security numbers, telephone, street, house, license, and credit card numbers. Your personal numbers are on your car, library card, laundry, insurance policies and church offering envelopes. You share a zip code, area code, congressional district, and voting precinct number with your neighbors. And there are many other numbers that each of us has attached to some part of our lives. Numbers have become essential to existence in this complex and crowded world.

But numbers are cold and impersonal. To sign a letter with a social security number, or any of the other dozens of numbers that could be traced to you, would hardly convey the personal warmth that your name does.

Names are intimate reflections of who we are and what we have come to mean to one another. Often a name has some special family significance. Often names are "inherited" and repeated from one generation to another. Sometimes when a child dies, the name is given to the next child to be born in the family. To inherit the name of a special person who has passed on, subtly imposes a bit of a burden. (I am well aware of this responsibility because my name first belonged to a sister who died several years before I was born.) To live up to the potential of the original holder of a name is difficult—if not impossible.

Names are significant. We want to retain our personal, private uniqueness, with our own distinctive names and personalities. But in our highly automated society dominated by computers there is the risk of becoming only a cipher.

A prominent German theologian, imprisoned for his political views during World War II, said that one of the most demeaning things about his imprisonment was to be deprived of his name and to be identified only by a prison number. When he was finally released, he said that one of the greatest things about freedom was being able to reclaim his own name. Then he felt that his personhood had been restored after the months of ignominy in prison.

Important as our own names are to us, the name of Jesus Christ is even more important.

Long before he was born, the prophet Isaiah wrote, "His name will be called Wonderful Counselor, Mighty God, Everlasting Father, Prince of Peace." These names helped describe the kind of person he would be and what his responsibilities would be.

When the angel told Mary that she would bear a Son, the angel said, "You shall call his name Jesus, for he will save his people from their sins."

Jesus accomplished what he was sent to do because he "humbled himself and became obedient unto death, even death on a cross." God rewarded him with honor and gave his name the greatest possible significance. Henceforth he would be Jesus, *the Lord*. When God raised Jesus from the dead, he confirmed the fact that Jesus was truly his Son, with access to all of God's power and resources. Jesus had done what God wanted him to do and the Father approved. From that point on, "at the name of Jesus every knee should bow, in heaven and on earth and under the earth, and every tongue confess that Jesus Christ is

85

Lord" (Phil. 2:10). He had earned the glory and honor due his name.

Although the people had treated Jesus as a common criminal dying in disgrace, his resurrection from the dead became the pivotal point of history. God had thus certified his divinity. Yet even with that miraculous event, it isn't easy to confess in sincerity that Jesus is Lord. In fact, according to 1 Cor. 12:3, "No one can say 'Jesus is Lord' except by the Holy Spirit."

The lordship of Christ is not something that one may discover from searching the records. The Holy Spirit must reveal it. To accept Jesus as Lord is to acknowledge his uniqueness, to give him unquestioned loyalty and allegiance, to obey his directions, and to love him without reservation. It means surrendering to his dominion and direction. It means that those who are identified with him will follow where he leads.

Claiming the name of Jesus, we may be ridiculed or we may be persecuted. But we must not let that intimidate us. "If you are reproached for the name of Christ, you are blessed, because the spirit of glory and of God rests upon you."

The name of Jesus has great power. It can be the source of physical health and healing as it was for the crippled beggar to whom Peter said, "I have no silver or gold, but I give you what I have; in the name of Jesus Christ of Nazareth, walk." Later Peter told the crowd, "And his name, by faith in his name, has made this man strong . . . the faith which is through Jesus has given the man this perfect health" (Acts 3).

Even more important than this, however, is that only in the name of Jesus will be we saved from eternal damnation. "There is . . . salvation in no one else, for there is no other name under heaven given among men by which we must be saved."

In the name of Jesus we are assured of eternal life. "I write this to you who believe in the name of the Son of God, that you may *know* that you have eternal life."

Read John 3

Thank God for Jesus Christ, his only begotten Son, who was willing to give up his glory in heaven to become one of us. Thank God that you have such a Savior. Tell him what Jesus means to you. Ask God how your life and witness may be more effective so that others whose lives touch yours may be assured of their eternal salvation.

25

Handling Anger

Someone says something thoughtless, and it hurts your feelings. Immediately anger flares up within you. Your muscles tense. You want to strike back somehow, perhaps by saying something hurtful. But fortunately, you don't trust yourself to talk at that moment of emotion. You just want to get off by yourself and brood about the insulting words that had aroused this flash of anger in you.

You would like to find some way to retaliate, to hurt as you have been hurt. But, at the moment, you don't even trust yourself to speak.

Anger is a disastrous emotion which can disturb us so much we can't think clearly. Anger makes us say and do things that we are certain to regret later. Sometimes we feel paralyzed with helpless rage.

Anger is a tricky emotion. It can make us do ridiculous things. It makes us want to strike back and hurt someone else as we have been hurt. It has been said that the measure of a person is the size of the thing it takes to "get his goat." Some people delight in prodding others until they reach that level of irritation. Most of us are sensitive to criticism, unkind or threatening words; when they are directed toward us, anger quickly flares up. Hurt pride makes us both defensive and aggressive.

Nasty as it is, however, anger is a valid emotion—it is not all bad. We should be angry at injustice and unfairness. We may need to use that powerful emotion of anger to combat overt indecency. Anger flares most quickly and most violently when we feel that we have personally been treated unjustly.

Jesus was capable of anger. He once took a whip and drove out the merchants who were desecrating the temple. His was righteous anger, and there are times when we ought to be angry.

Normally, however, when we succumb to anger our actions are usually not Christ-like. More likely we are acting like peevish children.

Anger is a very costly emotion. It inevitably takes a toll of our peace of mind. When we calm down, we usually regret that we did not control ourselves, and we feel embarrassed that we have publicly displayed the fact.

Jesus had three suggestions for handling anger. He said, "Agree quickly with your adversary." That sounds easy, but it may require overcoming pride in order to graciously permit the other person to do what he thinks best.

Jesus' second suggestion was, "Resist not evil." We may not personally be able to change a bad situation. There are other resources, not least of which is prayer. God can change things in his own way and in his own time if we ask him.

It takes real Christian maturity to be able to "bless those who curse you." It will surprise your adversary to find that you are willing to cooperate—as far as your conscience will permit— and that may be a great deal farther than he had expected.

It has been suggested that the most disarming thing we can do to the enemy is to be aggressively kind rather than to resist. In this way the situation can be subtly switched. If the aggressor is disarmed by kindness, he will not be quite sure how to handle the situation.

Anger is a strong emotion—so strong that it takes skill to

handle it wisely. God is stronger than our anger, and he can give us skill and wisdom for the proper use of our anger.

Read Ephesians 5

Thank God for your emotions. Ask him to help you tame and control your emotions and keep you from resentment. Ask for the grace to be kind to one another—even when people annoy you and seem to be determined to make life miserable for you. Ask God to forgive your impatience and intolerance and to give you the grace of forgiveness.

26

The Lord Looks at the Heart

Few of us are really satisfied with the way we look. We always think there could have been a better job done on us in the first place when our bones and flesh were put together. Advertising is deliberately geared to make us dissatisfied with the way we look. It convinces us that we ought to conform to more ideal proportions, but unfortunately few of us do. This becomes so discouraging that some people will starve themselves into ill health in order to achieve what is considered the ideal figure. Others will feel so defeated from the start that they ignore good health to eat what they want, and they avoid exercise like the plague.

But overweight is not the only problem. Some are concerned about being too tall, and others stand tall to appear closer to model proportions. There is a measure of comfort in Scripture that says, "Which of you by taking thought can add one cubit to his stature?" This same verse in some of the more modern versions reads: "Can any of you, however much he worries, make himself an inch taller?" (Matt. 6:27, Phillips).

Of course, the Lord expects us to exert reasonable care for our health by making right choices about what foods we eat and in what quantities. We are to take care of our physical bodies by plenty of rest, the right nourishing foods, and proper exercise. This is a matter of good stewardship because the greatest, most personal gift God has given us is our bodies.

In 1 Sam. 16:7 there is this comforting reassurance, "The Lord sees not as man sees; man looks on the outward appearance but the Lord looks on the heart."

True beauty is an internal matter. We can purchase pseudo-beauty in any store. The beauty that matters is the spirit and the personality. What we are on the inside will, of course, show through. No superficial cleansing, no external applications, no expensive beauty treatments are going to change what we are in the depth of our personal souls.

1 Peter 3:3-4 says, "Your beauty should not be dependent on an elaborate hairdo, or on the wearing of jewelry or fine clothes, but on the inner personality, on the unfading loveliness of a calm and gentle spirit, a thing very precious in the eyes of God" (Phillips).

How tall you are or how short, how much overweight you are or how skinny, the color of your hair and the cut of your clothes—none of these things matter as much as the unfailing, unfading loveliness of the inner person and spirit. The Lord doesn't see us in the same way that people do. They can only see the outside, but God looks at the heart. The truly important dimensions for the Christian are: How *deep* is your faith? How *high* is your hope. How *wide* is your love?

Read 1 Peter 1:13-25

Thank God for life, health, strength, and his promise of eternal life. Ask him to protect and keep you this day in good health so that you will be able to do the tasks which are yours with joy and satisfaction. Thank him again for his daily provision for all your needs.

27

Created to Create

Sometimes it seems that the tedious routine of a job is more than can be endured. The repetitiousness of work that is never finished becomes almost unbearably monotonous. How many times must the same dishes be washed and the same carpeting vacuumed or the same clothes washed? Often it is not the difficulty of work that annoys us as much as its constant repetition.

In the office, too, there are tasks that call for the same monotonous repetition—over and over again. It can be depressing, if you let yourself dwell on the routine repetitiveness of most of life's daily tasks.

But there is no way to avoid many of these repetitive duties if we are going to keep things going, maintain order, and avoid chaos both in the home and on the job. Postponing the tedious tasks and letting them pile up in the end makes them become even more onerous and unpleasant. If they are done in the first place when they should be taken care of, it will allow for more pleasant and satisfying pursuits and hobbies.

Whatever your attitude toward maintenance of self, family, and home, having some work to do and the ability to do it is certainly a blessing from God. Work provides an opportunity to develop and use skills, to express personal ideas, to release creative energies. At the same time it helps to keep order and cleanliness in the environment and a proper setting for happy living. The attitude in which we approach our necessary routine tasks can make a great deal of difference in how well we do what must be done, and how creatively we use time that is left over for personal pursuits, hobbies, and other creative expression.

Everyone has some abilities, but discovering them may take the courage. We never really know what we can do or how much we can accomplish until we try. Our first feeble efforts may not be too impressive, and they may convince us that our talents lie in another direction altogether. But trying something new may open a whole new area of satisfying activity. To deny that we have any personal gifts or talents is really to insult God, who has equipped us with the potential of being his partner in creation as we find ways to use his many gifts in our own creative ways. God has given all persons the potential to be creative in one way or another.

Talents never come to anyone full-blown. First, we may have only a glimmer of an interest in something. After a little study, some hard work, and perhaps a few dismal failures, our persistence will be rewarded by seeing a project accomplished. As we use our energies and devote our attention to learning more skills, we may be surprised by what we actually can do. But first we have to start, we have to try.

Most people are at least subconsciously aware that they are responsible for the prudent use of their financial resources. However, they may not always realize that they have a similar responsibility for the talents and skills that God has given them. Never make the mistake of thinking that the gifts of God are all in the area of producing *things* or in public presentations. Talents are also evident in the area of love and friendliness.

God, the Creator of us all, has provided us with the raw materials with which he expects us to live our lives in both comfort and joy. He is not interested only in our spiritual lives; he also wants us to use and appreciate all his good gifts, which can turn even the routine, necessary work of life into an exciting and rewarding adventure.

God understands about work. He made the world and everything in it. He gave us a whole world full of resources to enjoy, and he gave each person the marvelous gift of imagination. We can participate in the continuing creation as we use our gifts and talents. We were created to create, and few things can bring us as much satisfaction of using our own imaginations creatively. We are the children of a Creative Father who wants us also to enjoy our own creativity.

Read Romans 12:3-8

Thank God for your life and for his gifts of intellect, emotion, and skills. Ask him to reveal how you can make better use of these gifts. Pray for the courage to try new things that can give you a sense of creative accomplishment. Thank God for providing the raw materials of talent, time, and energy. Ask him to help you discover and acknowledge your personal gifts. He will bless you as you use them to create something of beauty.

28

Remember Whose You Are

Considering the pressures that most of us live under, it is easy to begin to complain about having too much to do and too little time to do it. We easily begin to fret about things that don't get done, things that happen which we didn't expect, and the dire consequences that might result if we don't accomplish all the things we think absolutely need to be done. A lot of emotional energy is dissipated in fretting.

When the pressure of too much to do is upon us, we often lose our self-control. Sometimes we even resort to tears of frustration and self-pity. How great it would be if one could always maintain a serene, calm attitude characterized by graciousness and poise! But, being very human, we lose that ideal emotional stance, and when the unlovely flare-up is over, we usually are filled with remorse.

Jesus was a model of serenity. He was self-confident, poised, unruffled—even under the most difficult pressures. He was exposed to unkind remarks, ridicule, testing, questioning—more than most of us will ever experience. But, knowing *who he was,* he didn't worry about losing status by the taunts of his critics.

Perhaps the key to maintaining such ideal poise and serenity may be indicated by Isaiah 26:3: "Thou dost keep him in perfect peace, whose mind is stayed on thee."

If we would take our eyes off ourselves and quit worrying about little hurts and insults, we could ride above the "slings and arrows" that come our way. Of course, sometimes we deserve the criticism we receive, for we have not done our best and we have let laziness or unconcern keep us from the loving deeds and the kind of words that would make a difference in our relationships. No matter how busy and absorbed we are with our own concerns and tasks, we ought not to lose touch with people around us. We should make the effort to be interested in the concerns of other people and compassionate for their hurts. What a difference it would make in our interpersonal relations if we would "live together in harmony, live together in love, as though we had only one mind and one spirit" (Phil. 2:4, Phillips).

But, unfortunately, when life presses in upon us and we feel overburdened with our own concerns, we ignore the concerns of others. We forget who we are and what God has promised to those who are his own.

We are a unique people: we who are Christians. We have been called to serve one another with love, but when we let the world "squeeze us into its mold" and "self" asserts itself, the good that we should do for one another is forgotten.

I bought a beautiful box of strawberries one day and looked forward to enjoying them at dinner. But unfortunately they were not what they appeared to be. There were a few lovely berries on top of the box, but underneath some were unripe and many were spoiled. If Christians, especially those to whom others look for leadership, are not sincere, genuine, and honest in all phases of their lives and in all contacts with others—like the strawberries, they are deceptive and worthless.

Romans 12:9 says, "Let us have no imitation Christian love. Let us have a genuine break with evil and a real devotion to good. Let us have real warm affection for one another as between brothers, and a willingness to let the other man have the credit" (Phillips).

I read an article entitled "Not Good If Detached." The author compared our Sunday life and our weekday life to the two parts of a bus ticket. There should be a continuity and a consistency that carries over from one to the other. We can't be one kind of person to our working associates and another kind of person to our families. Phil. 1:27 advises, "Make sure that your everyday life is worthy of the Gospel of Christ" (Phillips).

Perhaps we will always have too much to do and too little time to do it. We may never be able to escape the pressures and demands other people put upon us. But, as Christians, we have a "high calling" as Paul says, and we ought to live lives that are worthy of that high calling.

The Apostle Paul wrote: "I pray that out of the glorious richness of his resources he will enable you to know the strength of the Spirit's inner resources—that Christ may actually live in your hearts by your faith. And I pray that you, firmly fixed in love yourselves, may be able to grasp (with all Christians) how wide and deep and long and high is the love of Christ" (Eph. 3:16-19, Phillips).

Read Colossians 1:1-24

Ask God for the grace to accept your lot in life with patience, and to be at peace with those whose lives touch yours. Thank God for friends and family who help you to be all you can be.

29

Who Touched Me?

The world is a crowded place. We are constantly rubbing elbows with other people—those who are near and dear to us because of special relationships and also the many others we do not know personally but with whom we seem to be in subtle competition for living space.

In the larger cities we move through the streets and the labyrinth of buildings dodging one another, occasionally bumping in passing, but so absorbed in our own pursuits that we pay little heed to the masses. We are aware of the crowd of persons as an impediment and a nuisance congesting the area, rather than as real people with their own unique goals, ambitions, and needs.

After Jesus began his public ministry, he was followed by mobs of people—needy people, hurting people, curious people —who wondered about this unusual man who seemed not to fit into their expectations. Word about his unusual behavior, his gentleness, his strange ability to remain calm and unruffled under pressure, his miraculous healings had caused many to be curious about him. They wanted to know more about this strange man, whose teachings and conversation was so different, perhaps even heretical. Wherever he went, his reputation preceded him. People wanted to see for themselves what kind of a man this was who told simple stories that left them with deep questions about their own inner motivations and behavior.

Who was this man who had the strange power to drive out demons? They had heard about the Gerasene man. Everyone thought the man was crazy—but Jesus spoke just a few words and the demons which had plagued the man were driven out and into a farmer's pigs. All over the area the story was told how the pigs had rushed wildly down the steep bank to drown in the lake. As the story was repeated, the people were frightened, but they were also curious to see Jesus, hopeful that he would again demonstrate his magical powers.

The people had mixed emotions about Jesus. They wondered what he might do next; they had awe for anyone who was fearless and brash enough to defy the public authorities; and they were hoping for a chance to see him do another miracle. It would make a good show and bring some excitement into their tedious lives. So the crowds had eagerly gathered on the hillside to see Jesus and the disciples when they arrived.

Characteristically, Jesus used the occasion to teach. Out of compassion for the people's hunger, Jesus miraculously multiplied the limited resources to provide enough bread and fish to satisfy all the people who had followed him out of the city.

Another time when Jesus was walking through a small village, the usual crowd gathered, pressing around him until he was almost immobilized.

Suddenly Jesus asked, "Who touched me?" The question seemed ridiculous because so many people were crowding around him. But from a gentle grasp on the hem of his garment Jesus sensed that one person in the curious crowd had a deep need. So Jesus responded by healing the woman. The people were amazed.

Our lives are continually touching—in one way or another. People crowd around us on all sides. Mostly we try to ignore

100

these strangers and are unconcerned about their personal needs. But sometimes God works his miracles through the invisible force of influence. He sets each of us in the midst of a network of people. Whether we realize it or not, we leave our particular touch on the people with whom we rub elbows.

Some people, of course, are engaged in touching lives with healing, with teaching, with caring for human welfare. But this is what we are here for—to touch one another, to touch things, to touch situations and to make them better. Jesus used this simple method of reaching people. He picked a few men to be with him. He touched their lives, and he depended on them to reach out and touch the lives of others.

Sometimes we push, pull, or even shove people around—not to be helpful and to bring healing, but rather to just get them out of our way. One day there was a blind man standing hesitantly on the street corner. A man eager to help came up and grabbed his arm, and began to pull him across the street. The blind man braced himself and said, "Please, don't pull me or push me—all I need is the touch of your hand on my shoulder."

We have the potential for being helpful to one another. We can share our strength, our vision, our gifts, and our talents—but we must do it gently, not forcing ourselves and our abilities on others, but being thoughtful and considerate of them.

All of us have been touched by many persons—our parents, our friends, our working companions, and casual acquaintances whose lives and interests have somehow meshed with ours. It is important to be helpful, to be supportive to all whose lives in one way or another touch ours—but we must be gentle.

Read Luke 8:42b-48

Pray for grace to touch with gentleness the persons with whom you live and work. Ask for the insight to recognize needs in those around you and to find ways to relate helpfully. Thank God for persons whose lives have touched yours and left the mark of love upon you.

30

Be Yourself!

"It is not what you have but what you do with what you have that makes the difference." Emerson wrote those words of wisdom to point up the fact that life does not come to us "ready-made," but we are given the raw material with which to mold and shape a life for ourselves. The secret of building a worthwhile life is to learn to use the raw materials we have in awareness of our stewardship responsibilities. God wants us to dedicate all that we are and all that we have to his purpose. Then he promises to bless us and make us effective.

Scientists tell us that a lump of coal and a diamond develop from exactly the same raw materials. What makes the difference is the way the atoms are arranged.

It would be ridiculous for a lump of coal to pose as a diamond —and likewise, a diamond cannot be used for fuel. There may be times when a lump of coal has far greater utility value than many diamonds. But as a symbol of enduring love, a diamond could not be replaced by its distant cousin, the lump of coal. Each has its unique value when it performs the special function for which God created it.

Someone wisely has said, "If you want to be original, be

yourself. God never makes any duplicate copies!" Be yourself! Cease straining to copy and surpass other people. Settle down to the serious business of living your *own* life, using and developing your *own* gifts to the utmost.

Peter once asked Jesus about John's duties and activities in the kingdom. The answer Jesus gave to Peter was direct and positive: "What is that to you? Follow me!" (John 21:22).

Don't allow yourself to be disturbed by what others are doing. Your first obligation is to do your own thing—whatever it is—in the sphere where you are placed and to do it in the very best way possible. It was as though Jesus was saying, "Let John and me worry about what John is going to do. You have your own tasks. Follow me!"

Look at yourself. What do you have to work with? What talents do you have? What skills might still be discovered? What opportunities do you have—right where you are—to use special gifts? Don't deny that you have gifts. Make an honest inventory of yourself and your possibilities. It may surprise you!

Whether we are destined to be diamonds or lumps of coal, our significance in life depends on the use we make of the gifts God has given us. But either a diamond or a lump of coal serves no purpose whatsoever if they have not been unearthed. What gifts are hidden in you?

One who has dedicated herself and all that she has to the service of the Lord and his people will find plenty to do. This may mean the full utilization of all the gifts you have and all the raw material of your life. To be yourself is not only a matter of doing uncommon things. It is a matter of doing common things uncommonly well. When we are conscious of our stewardship obligation to serve one another and to serve God, using whatever gifts that God has given us, our service will be blessed and increased.

"Naturally there are different gifts and functions; individually grace is given to us in different ways out of the rich diversity of Christ's giving. . . . His gifts were made that Christians might

104

be properly equipped for their service, that the whole body might be built up until the time comes when, in the unity of common faith and common knowledge of the Son of God, we arrive at real maturity—that measure of development which is meant by 'the fullness of Christ' " (Eph. 4:7, 12-13, Phillips).

Be satisfied to be what God wants you to be, to live where he wants you to live, and be aware of the needs of all whose lives surround you. Help others to be all they can be, but remember, first of all, to *be yourself,* use your gifts of personality, talent, and possessions and reach out to others in love.

Read Romans 8

Thank God for life, health, strength. Ask him to help you recognize your unique gifts that they might be used lovingly to help others become all they can be. Seek ways to help others recognize their unique gifts. Help them to find creative ways to use and develop their best abilities as they find ways to serve one another.

31

God Is Not Deaf

"God is not deaf," a friend once said. "We don't have to keep repeating our requests over and over again. If we ask once, God remembers. He knows our need and will answer when we are ready to receive the answer."

That's good news, and it sounds logical enough. When we wonder whether or not he will hear and answer, perhaps we do not credit God with a memory and sufficient interest in our needs. Perhaps our prayer lives would have wider scope if we didn't dwell continually on our "pet petitions." Maybe we have not really understood what prayer is. Prayer is not just an order blank on which to list our wants. Properly understood, prayer is communion—a conversation with our heavenly Father with whom to talk things over, share our concerns, express our needs, and tell him how much we love and respect him. There are many good reasons for talking with our heavenly Father other than just asking him for what we want—although he does indeed encourage us to let him know what we feel will make life more rich and full for us.

There are some very good reasons for being persistent in prayer. In the first place, repeating the same request may help us see the folly of some of our desires. Some things we ask are selfish—even sinful. To bring our desires out for scrutiny before the throne of grace may help us recognize the pettiness and selfishness of many of our requests. Then we may have a chance to eliminate foolish, selfish petitions in favor of other more important, far-reaching prayer concerns.

Repetition of a prayer request also has the effect of focusing our own attention on our need. Then we can sort out our priorities and coordinate the energies of our bodies, minds, and spirits so that we can use our own strengths to bring about the answers we desire. When our own creative energies are directed in the proper channels, we are enabled at times to bring about the answers to our own prayers. Prayer is not just a market list, it is a creative force that can appropriate our own energies for effective results. At the same time prayer makes us more conscious of God's power and his support and encouragement.

We think that by persistence our prayers will be more likely to "get through" and capture the attention of God. But God is not reluctant, nor does he need to be cajoled into responding to our pleas. He is a generous and loving Father, but he wants us to grow up and to become resourceful in the use of our own talents and abilities. He does not want us to be spoiled children who ask for and receive everything they want from an indulgent parent. Through our prayers God can firm up our resolve and motivate us to use our own best intelligence and energies to solve our own problems.

But more than being a resource to help us and to provide for us, God is a loving Father who longs for communication with his children. He wants to hear us, to be reassured that we love him, and he appreciates evidence of gratitude for his goodness.

As the discussion of prayer with my friend ran on, we both aired our own understanding of prayer—what it is, how it works, how we can appropriate its power. We also shared experiences of amazing answers to our prayers. Then we decided to check again to see what Jesus has said about prayer.

107

First, we found that Jesus made a very definite distinction between *persistence* in prayer and what he calls "heaping up empty phrases." He said, "And in praying, do not heap up empty phrases, as the Gentiles do, for they think that they will be heard for their many words . . . . the Father knows what you need before you ask him" (Matt. 6:7-8).

But Jesus encouraged us to pray without ceasing, to bring our anxieties and needs to God, to be always in touch with him in full confidence that he hears, he cares, and will respond when we pray.

In Luke 18:1-8 Jesus is recorded as telling a parable to the effect that we ought always to pray and not to lose heart. To amplify that point he told a story about the widow who kept coming back to the judge begging him to vindicate her against her adversary. For a while the judge was annoyed and seemed inclined to refuse. But after her repeated pleas, he realized she was not going to give up, so he finally agreed to her request.

God is not deaf. He is not unwilling to listen, nor is he unconcerned about our problems. Jesus assured us many times that God cares, he listens, and he will act on our behalf. In John 11:41, speaking to God in prayer, Jesus said, "Father, I thank thee that thou hast heard me. I know that thou hearest me always."

God will also hear us when we pray. He is there, ready and waiting for us to ask for what we need. "Have no anxiety about anything, but in everything by prayer and supplication with thanksgiving let your requests be made known to God. And the peace of God, which passes all understanding, will keep your hearts and your minds in Christ Jesus" (Phil. 4:6).

Read Philippians 4

Thank God for the privilege of prayer. Learn to know him and to trust him as your heavenly Father who cares for your every need. He will guide, direct, encourage, support, and protect you through all of life's trials.

108

32

When I Am Afraid

In the shopping center one day two senior citizens were overheard reacting to a couple of young people who were wearing quite outlandish clothing. "My stars!" the one elderly lady said. "Am I ever glad that I'm not living in this day and age!"

Reading the daily paper could very well bring on the same reaction. Stories of crime, murder, robbery, atrocities, and degradation seem to dominate the news. Times have not changed much over the centuries. It is interesting to note that in Psalm 55 David writes about the horrors of life in that day:

"My heart is in anguish within me, the terrors of death have fallen upon me. Fear and trembling come upon me, and horror overwhelms me. And I say, 'O that I had wings like a dove! I would fly away and be at rest; yea, I would wander afar, I would lodge in the wilderness, I would haste to find me a shelter from the raging wind and tempest . . . . for I see violence and strife in the city. Day and night they go around it on its walls; and mischief and trouble are within it, ruin is in its midst; oppression and fraud do not depart from its market place. . . . Destroy their plans, O Lord, confuse their tongues.' "

The violence and strife, the mischief and trouble in our present day also strike terror in the hearts of the people who want to live safely in our cities. Every day the newspaper reports atrocities that shock and disturb peace-loving citizens. Yet it is amazing how placid we can be in the face of these horrible things. We become really disturbed and concerned when such things get so close that we feel personally threatened. Then we panic.

Life is full of trials and tribulations. Like the psalmist, we too may often look for a way to escape from the threatening situations with which we live. But also, like David, we have to admit that escape is not really very easy. David's personal expression of trust gives us inspiration, "When I am afraid, I put my trust in thee. In God, whose word I praise, in God I trust without a fear. What can flesh do to me?" (Psalm 56:3-4).

But somehow David's trust seems naive. We want to *do* something, or get someone in authority to do something about a bad situation. The more courageous among us want to rush out and change things or at least get into the fight for civil rights and see what can be done to correct a bad situation.

There is something to be said for activism, but it can so easily make an already bad situation worse. To try to "fight fire with fire" or to strike back when we have been struck may only add violence to violence. From this there is no end.

It is encouraging to read Psalm 55 and 56, where the psalmist answers his own anxiety, "But I call upon God and the Lord will save me. . . . Cast your burden on the Lord, and he will sustain you; he will never permit the righteous to be moved. . . . This I know, God is for me."

Over and over again the psalmist reiterates his confidence in the steadfast love of God which will protect from all adversity. With the power of God working on our behalf, why should we fear?

To read this portion in full awareness that many martyrs have died for the faith may raise doubts about the promises of God to protect his own and to be with them whatever happens. But the record of how the martyrs were given strength to endure

110

what happened to them—even unto death—tells us that they faced persecution and even death in complete confidence that God was with them, sustaining them in pain and taking them through the gates of death into the kingdom of heaven.

The Lord Jesus became man to demonstrate God's love and to show us how to live in loving relationship with all persons. He showed us God's compassion when he taught us to pray; he opened heaven's treasure-store for our use.

If we ask him, God will supply every need of ours according to his riches in glory through Christ Jesus.

Read Psalm 55 and 56

Thank God for every evidence of his care and protection. Trust him with your anxieties, confident that he can give you courage for whatever you must face as you live out your days in the midst of a crooked and perverse generation. God is merciful to his own. Trust him.